To: James & Rebecca
with lots & lots
of love to our
bestest friends
xxx

EUROPE

Rising
Fashion
Designers

PATRICK GOTTELIER

Schiffer Publishing Ltd®

4880 Lower Valley Road • Atglen, PA 19310

Dedicated to Jane who, having dragged me into the fashion industry, has watched with amused tolerance as I have extracted more fun from the fashion roller coaster than should be legal!

ACKNOWLEDGMENTS

Firstly my thanks to Jo Davis who first recommended me to Schiffer publishing as being a suitable "case" for consideration as compiler of this book.. This also gives me the opportunity to publicly recognize the ground breaking work Jo did behind the scenes way back in the 1980s to forge a bunch of disparate designers and organizations into one central exhibition venue and thereby lay the foundations for that creative vortex known as London Fashion Week.

Thanks must also go to Sally Congdon-Martin for leading the way in the USA with *Emerging Fashion Designers 1*, which created the context for this book and Jeff Snyder my editor for his patience, understanding, and support.

The book would simply not have been possible without the sterling (and charming) research carried out on my behalf by Jo Thomas and would probably not be being read by you now if it were not for the additional research contribution made by Angie Noon. I would also like to thank David Hawkins associate Dean of research and Innovation at University College Falmouth for helping me frame the academic context of this book. I am deeply grateful and indebted to them all.

Of course, the book could not have happened at all without the support of the contacts at the contributing institutions; many of them friends from my many years in the industry, all of them have been exceptionally supportive at busy times in their own schedules. Forgive me for all those years I worked in the industry making light of your efforts in education. I now know just how hard you all work and how dedicated you are to your students.

Finally I must thank my own Colleagues at University College Falmouth who have encouraged me to develop my own research by allowing and supported me in carving out the time to put this book together. A very special Arts institution with an illustrious past and a glittering future.

CONTENTS

INTRODUCTION

As a student at the Central School of Art and Design I remember my first sightings of the fashion students across the way at St. Martins School of Art and being in awe of the creativity, passion, and drive of fashion designer undergraduates. In the early days I would just look and be amazed and didn't initially even realize that I was slowly (at first) being drawn into that world. Perhaps my route to the heart of the Fashion Industry was sufficiently circuitous to mask the inevitability of the destination. One of the St. Martins students was Jane Foster who became my partner and I was drawn down an invisible path from designing exercise toys for children with Myelomeningocele, to inflatable welded jackets to making costume for science fiction then theatre and finally real clothes. I mention all this because through the process of eventually running a fashion house I became distanced from the creative powerhouse that is, at its best at the core of a fashion department.

Now that I am again working in a creative institution and have the privilege of working with young fashion undergraduates I am reminded of the powerhouse of creativity they can constitute, but something has changed. The optimism, the energy, the passion, and the work ethic are all still part of the DNA, but now there is a greater understanding of the responsibility for and willingness to address the ecological, sustainability ethical issues we all face.

The young fashion designers represented on the pages of this book are poised to become not just the style setters but the opinion formers and drivers for social change in our society. From that perspective alone the book should be viewed and interpreted by anyone interested in the broader aspect of our society's future. There continues to be a tension between aspirations to be responsible, desire to have fun and be creative, and the realities and challenges of everyday life. The emerging fashion designers in this book display tendencies to all three factions and more, but what is really interesting in my view is the creativity with which those issues are addressed and the emerging revelation of a once invisible pathway.

NOTE ON THE BOOK'S METHODOLOGY:

This volume has been produced as a selected catalogue of the most interesting work produced in the last year by the foremost fashion design education programmes in Europe. The institutions featured have alumni with significant track records in garment design and production and have been influential in developing Europe's fashion industry as one of the largest and most influential in the world.

The selection process for inclusion began by consulting expert opinion from a broad range of professionals connected with the fashion industry, including academics, designers, fashion promoters, fashion buyers, heads of fashion houses, writers, and critics. The expert group was asked to articulate, using their own criteria, how they would evaluate the best fashion courses in Europe, then to use these to produce a long list of the premier programs. This produced a diverse range of responses, including economic criteria, the influence of alumni, the opinion of trade professionals over a number of years, and their popularity with students and potential students. The criteria were collated to form a basis for the final short-listing of programs. The size of the shortlist was determined both by the degree of overlap in the expert long-listing process and by the intended size of the publication. Many institutions were cited by multiple experts using similar criteria, making their inclusion straightforward. Other choices, where there was slightly less support for inclusion, were made by comparing the standard of student work submitted using the same criteria used to determine which work was to be included from the institutions first identified.

After making an initial selection, the institutions short-listed were contacted to request material that could be selected for inclusion in the book. It was interesting to note that there was a strong correlation between the perceived reputations of institutions – as judged by the panel of experts – and the quantity of material submitted. The task of gathering material from programme teams was, however, made both more challenging and more interesting by the wide diversity of titles used by institutions to describe those managing them.

The criteria used by the expert team, tempered by my own industry and academic experience, gave me the basis for editorial judgments about the inclusion of individual pieces of student work. Of particular concern were the context for the production of the work, the intentions of the designer, and how successfully they had fulfilled that intention, all balanced against likely industry perceptions and the history of fashion production in Europe.

Work submitted by institutions was intended by them to represent the best of their current output when assessed both in terms of their internal academic criteria and a judgment made by the programme teams about those pieces that would be most suitable for inclusion in this publication. Academic judgments are made in relation to the intended learning outcomes of programmes, however, this book has used selection criteria based on a broader industry context and editorial decisions have been made to achieve balance in the volume.

There is significant debate over the nature of judgments made in academic contexts - to what extent they are subjective or objective - and the match between those qualities sought in student work compared to industry-led criteria. The selection process for this volume has attempted to take into account both academic and industrial contexts and to ensure that selections have been made that acknowledge both.

ANNE BOSMAN

**Fashion Design BA
ArtEZ Institute of the
Arts, Arnhem**
Home town/Country:
Deventer, The
Netherlands

Fashion Design:
Menswear

Inspiration:
The collection is based
on a portrait series
of sitting Japanese
emperors with their
kimonos folded like three-
dimensional pieces
of art. This reminded
me of children who
wrap fabrics around
their bodies and create
their own sculptures.
I used this way of
thinking to research new
silhouettes.

Graduation/Awards:
Cum Laude
Finalist at the Frans
Molenaar Couture
Award 2011

Advised by:
Matthijs Boelee,
course director,
Fashion Design,
ArtEZ Institute of
the Arts, Arnhem

Silk gazar, polyester fleece, bias-cut cotton, cotton jersey,
cotton canvas, screenprint. *Photography by Peter Stigter*

:: Silk, cotton terry, cotton denim, linen, leather. *Photography by Peter Stigter*

:: Cotton molton, cotton gabardine, viscose, silk/linen blend, cotton canvas, digital print, polystyrene. *Photography by Peter Stigter*

:: Cotton, digital print, polystyrene. *Photography by Peter Stigter*

:: Polyester, cotton/ polyester blend, cotton, cotton canvas, digital print. *Photography by Peter Stigter*

LINDA DE JONG

**Fashion Design BA
ArtEZ Institute of the
Arts, Arnhem**
Home town/Country:
Amsterdam,
The Netherlands

Fashion Design:
Womenswear

Inspiration:
The collection is inspired
by the boundary that
separates fashion from
anti-fashion. Starting
points were the
combinations of various
garments and materials
as used by the African
women photographed
by Jacky Nickerson. I
used polypropylene as
a base and combined
this with mohair to make
new interpretations of
tweeds and pied-de-
cocks.

Graduation/Awards:
Cum Laude

Advised by:
Matthijs Boelee,
course director,
Fashion Design,
ArtEZ Institute of
the Arts, Arnhem

Mohair/polypropylene tweed, stone-washed silk.
Photography by Peter Stigter

:: Cupro,
mohair/flambé/
polypropylene tweed.
*Photography by
Peter Stigter*

:: Polypropylene/
viscose pied-de-cock,
stone-washed silk.
*Photography by
Peter Stigter*

:: Polypropylene/
viscose pied-de-cock,
polypropylene, silk,
stone-washed silk.
*Photography by
Peter Stigter*

:: Hand-knitted
flambé wool, viscose.
*Photography by
Peter Stigter*

MAGNUS DEKKER

**Fashion Design BA
ArtEZ Institute of the
Arts, Arnhem**
Home town/Country:
Arnhem, The
Netherlands

Fashion Design:
Womenswear

Inspiration:
My aim is to highlight the
flaws of modern fashion,
for they are to me what
makes fashion interesting
and very much alive.
For this collection, the
starting point was the
everlasting conflict
between the conformist
and the individual,
using influences from
conformist soccer and
award ribbons won on
individual merits.

Graduation/Awards:
Winner of the Frans
Molenaar Couture
Award 2011

Advised by:
Matthijs Boelee,
course director,
Fashion Design,
ArtEZ Institute of
the Arts, Arnhem

Silk moiré, polyester/cotton canvas, cotton jersey,
polyester, silk-screen printing, baby alpaca, feathers.
Photography by Peter Stigter

12

:: Mohair knit, silk moiré, vintage Dutch Navy blankets, embroidery. *Photography by Peter Stigter*

:: Polyester/cotton canvas, mohair knit, baby alpaca, polyester blankets. *Photography by Peter Stigter*

:: Mohair knit, polyester flags, moiré, alpaca wool. *Photography by Peter Stigter*

:: Woolen blanket, quilted nylon, embroidery, cotton Jersey, silk-screen printing, baby alpaca, polyester. *Photography by Peter Stigter*

MATTIA AKKERMANS

**Fashion Design BA
ArtEZ Institute for the
Arts, Arnhem**
Home town/Country:
Arnhem, The
Netherlands

Fashion Design
Womenswear

Inspiration:
This collection is based
on traditional costumes
from the Dutch province
Zeeland and colonial
Suriname from around
1900. A contradiction
to my first source of
inspiration—a video
by Ryoichi Kurokawa of
digitalized landscapes.
Both directions resulted
in a collection that
embodies a fascinating
clash between manual
and digital, between
tradition and the future.

Graduation/Awards:
Cum Laude
Nominated for
Lichting 2011 – G-Star
Raw Talent Award

Advised by:
Matthijs Boelee,
course director,
Fashion Design,
ArtEZ Institute of
the Arts Arnhem

Pink coated nylon with silk screen print, magenta linen
polyester with torn out threads, green linen with silk screen
print and embroidery. *Photography by Peter Stigter*

:: Magenta linen polyester with thorn out threads, hand-dyed yellow silk. *Photography by Peter Stigter*

:: Green silk with silk screen print, white polyester organza attached with special punch technique, white pineapple fabric with silk screen print, yellow cotton rayon with digital print and embroidery. *Photography by Peter Stigter*

:: Yellow polyester, green silk with silk screen print and embroidery, orange silk with silk screen print, pink nylon, dark pink rice fabric. *Photography by Peter Stigter*

:: Cotton rayon with digital print, red polyester organza attached with special punch technique, embroidery with fake hair and ostrich feathers, purple silk with silk screen print. *Photography by Peter Stigter*

SANNE SCHEPERS

**Fashion Design BA
ArtEZ Institute of the
Arts, Arnhem**
Home town/Country:
Arnhem, The
Netherlands

Fashion Design:
Womenswear

Inspiration:
My collection is based on
the principle of a twinset,
for which I developed
a reversible design
concept. By twisting half
of the garment inside-
out before cutting it
at two different points,
it becomes possible
to wear the designs
in four different ways.
Handmade finishing
defines the charisma of
this collection.

Graduation/Awards:
Cum Laude
Winner of Lichting
2011/G-Star Raw
Talent Award

Advised by:
Matthijs Boelee,
course director,
Fashion Design,
ArtEZ Institute of
the Arts, Arnhem

Woollen crepe, silk, hand-stitched satin and silk
ribbons, hand-stitched silk bias-binding, nylon.
Photography by Peter Stigter

:: Woollen crepe, wool, silk, hand-stitched silk and satin ribbons, hand-stitched silk bias-binding, nylon. *Photography by Peter Stigter*

:: Cotton, cool wool, hand-stitched satin ribbons, nylon. *Photography by Peter Stigter*

:: Cotton, woollen crepe, hand-stitched grosgrain and satin ribbons, nylon. *Photography by Peter Stigter*

:: Wool, woollen crepe, cotton, hand-stitched silk bias binding. *Photography by Peter Stigter*

MEGAN CORNWELL

**Fashion Studies
BA (Hons)
Arts University College,
Bournemouth**
Home town/Country: UK

Womenswear, print

Inspiration:
Final collection "F1,"
is based on race car
engineering. Inspiration
from the car structures are
used for pattern cutting
and photographs of car
headlights for the print
design.

Digital print dress. *Photography by Simon Armstrong*

:: Digital print dress with quilted metallic cropped jacket. *Photography by Simon Armstrong*

:: Digital print silk shirt with metallic thread wool skirt and jacket. *Photography by Simon Armstrong*

:: Contrast digital print trousers and silk shirt worn with metallic thread wool jacket. *Photography by Simon Armstrong*

:: Digital print silk dress with metallic leather engineer pleated cropped jacket. *Photography by Simon Armstrong*

CHELSEA GOSLING

**Fashion Studies
BA (Hons)
Arts University College,
Bournemouth**
Home town/Country: UK

Menswear

Inspiration:
Inspiration primarily from architectural surroundings, interpreted into shapes and textures for textile details; focusing on clean silhouettes with tactile qualities.

Heavy gauge funnel neck textured wool sweater.
Photography by Simon Armstrong

:: Pleated wool shirt with wide legged trousers. Laser cut suede throw. *Photography by Simon Armstrong*

:: Bonded double faced wool jacket with heavy wool collar. *Photography by Simon Armstrong*

:: Lined heavy cotton jacket with tweed wool collar. *Photography by Simon Armstrong*

:: Pleated shirt detail, wool trousers, heavy gauge tweed wool hooded collar piece. *Photography by Simon Armstrong*

CLARE HARMAN

**Fashion Studies
BA (Hons)
Arts University College,
Bournemouth**
Home town/Country: UK

Womenswear

Inspiration:
Exploration of the relationship between craft and technology, looking positively at the way they aid each other. Bold triangular prints complemented by soft smoky effects, matt and shiny, textured and soft; a culmination of opposites working together.

Engineer dyed dress with glazed leather jacket.
Photography by Simon Armstrong

:: Raw edged engineer dyed silk dress with glazed leather overdress. *Photography by Simon Armstrong*

:: Silk print top with glazed leather cropped jacket and trousers. *Photography by Simon Armstrong*

:: Print inspiration and concept board. *Photography by Clare Harman*

:: Complete Collection. *Photography by Simon Armstrong*

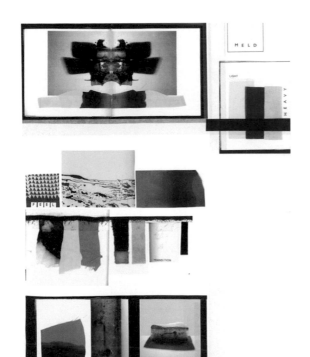

EVA LOJDOVA

**Fashion Studies
BA (Hons)
Arts University College,
Bournemouth**
Home town/Country: UK

Womenswear

Inspiration:
Designs developed from
an interest in pattern
and shape with strong
sculptural references.
Inspiration comes from
the juxtaposition of
textures and materials.

Hand printed pleat and folded waistcoat with
leather trousers and laser cut suede accessories.
Photography by Simon Armstrong

:: Glazed cotton hand printed complex fold coat with leather trousers. Laser cut accessories. *Photography by Simon Armstrong*

:: Pleat and fold glazed shirt worn with leather trousers. *Photography by Simon Armstrong*

:: Contrast lined hand printed fold coat with vibrant leather trousers. *Photography by Simon Armstrong*

:: Light silk hand printed sleeveless coat with leather trousers. Laser cut suede accessories. *Photography by Simon Armstrong*

RICKY MOAKES

**Fashion Studies
BA (Hons)
Arts University College,
Bournemouth**
Home town/Country: UK

Menswear

Inspiration:
The current collection
has personal references
and is playful, energetic,
loud, raw, oversized and
fresh.

Oversized cotton shirt with laser cut detailing and
graphic prints. Contrast stitched denim jeans.
Photography by Simon Armstrong

:: Graphic print cotton and knit T. Heavy denim coat with rope detailing. *Photography by Simon Armstrong*

:: Graphic print top, contrast stitch engineer cut denim trousers. *Photography by Simon Armstrong*

:: Laser cut detailing on shirt and denim coat with contrast stitching. *Photography by Simon Armstrong*

:: Laser cut detail on cotton shirt with contrast stitching. *Photography by Simon Armstrong*

ELLINOR KELLNER

**BA in Fashion
Beckmans
College of Design**
Home town/Country:
Stockholm, Sweden

Fashion Design

Inspiration:
The Standard
The collection examines
our aesthetic relationship
to pets. I have worked
with shapes that are
desirable in breeding
and have been inspired
by phenomena such
as pet grooming and
the use of pets as
accessories. Are these
shapes and expressions
still attractive if applied
to humans?

Advised by:
Göran Sundberg,
Course director/Senior
Lecturer in fashion
design. Beckmans
College of Design

Design: Ellinor Kellner. Photo: Marcus Palmqvist

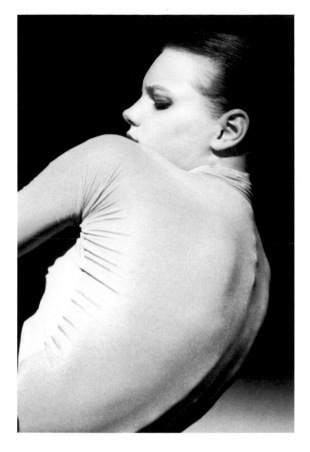

:: *Design: Ellinor Kellner. Photo: Marcus Palmqvist*

:: *Design: Ellinor Kellner. Photo: Marcus Palmqvist*

:: *Design: Ellinor Kellner. Photo: Marcus Palmqvist*

:: *Design: Ellinor Kellner. Photo: Marcus Palmqvist*

ISABELLE LUNDH

**BA in Fashion
Beckmans
College of Design**
Home town/Country:
Stockholm, Sweden

Fashion Design

Inspiration:
This is a manifestation for the identity and the self. For hidden values of attraction, the abstract embodiment of a person's character, invisible like an unspoken word, this formulates in my collection in freely painted UV patterns and fluorescent materials where hidden values can be seen only in the right lighting.

Graduation/Awards:
H&M premier scholarship holder, this collection.

Advised by:
Rebecca Lundh, artist, and her abstract paintings inspired this collection.

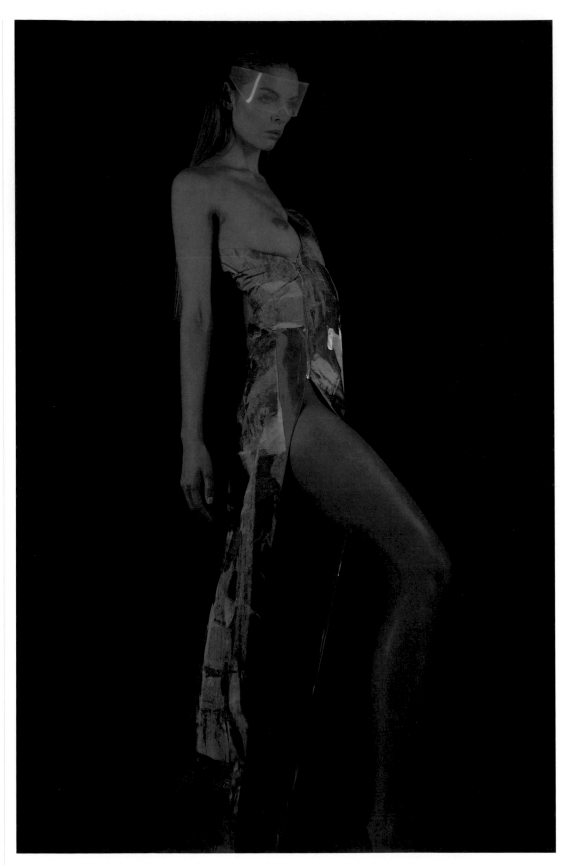

Dress in silk with UV-color pattern.
Photography by Alexander Dahl

:: Dress in silk with UV-color pattern. *Photography by Alexander Dahl*

:: Fluorescent asymmetric top. *Photography by Alexander Dahl*

:: Short jacket, yarn tied on leather. Fluorescent skirt. *Photography by Alexander Dahl*

:: Top in silk with UV-color pattern and asymmetric beige skirt. *Photography by Alexander Dahl*

MADELEINE VINTBACK

BA in Fashion
Beckmans
College of Design
Home town/Country:
Stockholm, Sweden

Inspiration:
What determines our perception of aesthetics? What separates the attractive from the unsightly? By manipulating elements which, at first glance, evoke negative associations —materials used to make Orthopedic braces, or materials that have been discarded—I have attempted to reconsecrate them, establishing these materials in a new context.

Graduation/Awards:
Ann Wall's design award 2011

Catsuit: mesh elastic bands.
Corset: vacuum formed plastic.
Shoes: vacuum formed plastic.
Photography by Simon Maddock

:: Top: non yellowing foam, mesh elastic bands. Trousers: translucent silicone. Shoes: vacuum formed plastic. *Photography by Simon Maddock*

:: Coat: plastic fur, deco gras. Shirt: silk. Trousers: silk. Shoes: vacuum formed plastic. *Photography by Simon Maddock*

:: Jacket: quilted, silicone coated. Trousers: Translucent polyethylene. Shoes: Vacuum formed plastic. *Photography by Simon Maddock*

:: Coat: Translucent polyethylene, silicone shoulder-pads. Trousers: three-dimensional knit spacer fabric. Top: Moiré pattern on Fiberglass fly screen. Shoes: Vacuum formed plastic. *Photography by Simon Maddock*

ALFHILD SARAH KÜLPER

BA Fashion
Womenswear
Central Saint Martins
Home town/Country:
Stockholm, Sweden

Fashion Design:
Womenswear

Inspiration:
For my collection I developed a technique to render 3D prints through layers of translucent fabrics. The prints include giant faces which are serious and challenging, as a reaction to a representation of women as pleasing towards or owned by the spectator. The more abstract silhouettes are inspired by my mother's performance acts.

Graduation/Awards:
First Degree Honors

Advised by:
Howard Tangye, Head of Womenswear at Central Saint Martins

Layered tulle with hand painted 3D prints and silk.
Photography by Clark Franklyn

:: Layered tulle with hand painted 3D prints. *Photography by Clark Franklyn*

:: Layered tulle with hand painted 3D prints. *Photography by Clark Franklyn*

:: Rubber foam jacket, layered tulle pants, lamé top. *Photography by Clark Franklyn*

:: Pen on paper

KIRSTY LONGMAN

Central Saint Martins
Home town/Country:
Gravesend, UK

Fashion:
Menswear

Inspiration:
My collection was based on a juxtaposition of two themes: utilitarian, combat clothing and old ladies' interior design choices. Somehow the dense floral patterns on the cheap synthetic fabrics of grandmothers' houses reminded me of the patterns found in camouflage designs and so GRANOUFLAGE was born.

Graduation/Awards:
First Class
honors degree

Advised by:
Christopher New

Look 1 - Curtains: Printed cotton/lino casual jacket with concealed placket pocket detail. Cotton, cross-stitch fabric, one-piece collar shirt. Pearl necklace.
Photography by Henna Mailk

:: Look 2 – Crafty Camo: Cotton intarsia jumper. Cotton "camo-cross-stitch" embroidered jogging bottoms. Embroidered cotton lace-up shoes. All embroidery/knit in same yarns. *Photography by Henna Mailk*

:: Look 3 – Aprons: Linen/cotton mix navy suit: two-button, concealed placket jacket with hidden placket pocket detail, slanted front pockets and shoulder "para" pockets. Apron-front trousers. Cotton, one-piece collar shirt with military construction hood. Cotton loafers. Pearl necklace. *Photography by Henna Mailk*

:: Look 4 - Tabards: Treated, nylon/cotton mix tabard with jersey rib details. Digital print, floral camouflage t-shirt in cotton interlock. Hand-printed, Soviet-style camouflage, cotton cross-stitch fabric jogging bottoms. Cotton, lace-up shoes. *Photography by Henna Mailk*

:: Look 5 - Cardi: Hand knitted (garter stitch) cardigan with rib collar and chain closure. Digital print, abstract camouflage tailored trousers. Digital print, floral, nylon t-shirt. *Photography by Henna Mailk*

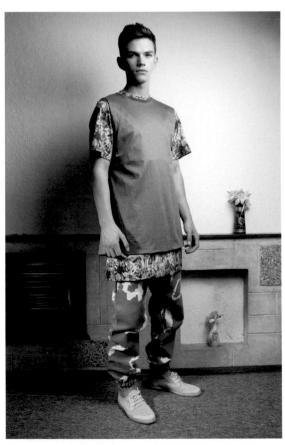

FLAMINIA SACCUCCI

**BA (Hons) Fashion Design Print
Central Saint Martins**
Home town/Country:
Rome, Italy

Fashion Print

Inspiration:
The collection is mainly made of screen-printed latex, mixed with digitally printed leather and tulle. The aim was to produce an unexpected use of latex, not expressly sexy, but with sharp and feminine silhouettes and prints. In order to achieve this femininity I used a softer garden landscape print to smooth the graphicity of the tyre.

Graduation/Awards:
L'Oréal Professionnel
   Talent Award, Best
   Collection of
   the Year 2011
Collection was
   nominated best
   among all Central
   Saint Martins
   graduates of 2011

Advised by:
Course Director
Willie Walters

Mixed Media—Pencil and Photoshop

∷ Screen printed latex

∷ Screen printed latex

∷ Paper cut out print
on tulle and screen
printed latex

∷ Screen printed latex

KIM TRAEGER

**BA (Honors) Fashion
with Knit Wear
Central Saint Martins**
Home town/Country:
Aabenraa, Denmark

Fashion Design:
Knitwear

Inspiration:
A rabbit is driven over by
a car when it crosses a
road at night. When it
stands with its intestines
in its paws it realizes it's
the Easter bunny. We
follow the bunny from
the accident until it's
patched together again
and can travel out into
the white forest.

Advised by:
Sarah Gresty

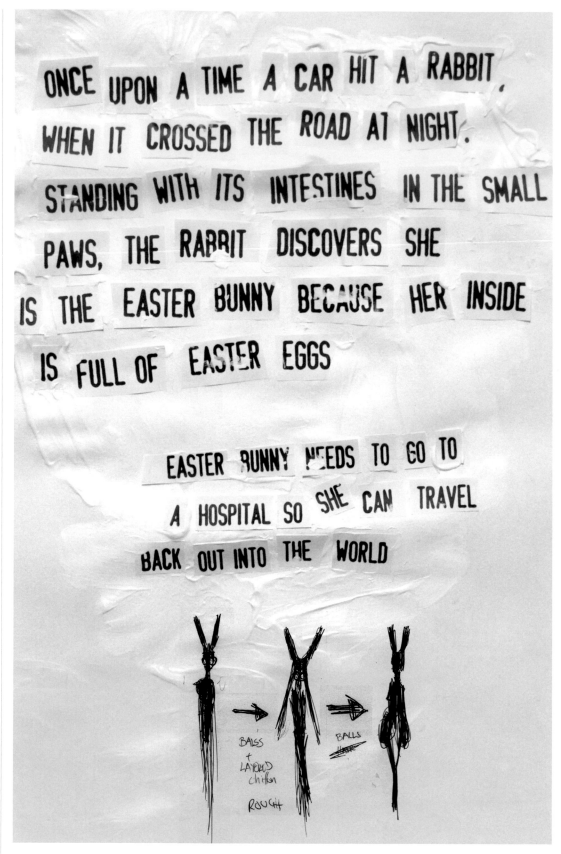

Mix media

40

:: Mixed media.

:: Jersey, pleated felt, painted and varnished crochet, painted woven leather. Mask, vacuum moulded plastic, laser cut plastic, embroidery.

:: Jersey, brushed knitted mohair, painted woven leather, laser cut leather, coated and broken leather. Mask, vacuum moulded plastic, laser cut plastic, embroidery.

:: Pleated felt, leather, knitted viscose, coated and broken leather, woven painted leather. Mask, vacuum moulded plastic, laser cut plastic, embroidery.

EMILY ANDREWS

BA Hons
Fashion Design
De Montfort University
Home town/Country:
Camberley Surrey,
United Kingdom

Fashion Design:
Womenswear

Inspiration:
My collection titled "I'll show you my dinosaur" is girly with a perverse twist, combining clashing concepts to create unexpected silhouettes and embellishment. It is inspired by American beauty pageants and childhood, juxtaposing perfect, shiny plastic against fragility and vulnerability. It is about layering awkward shapes with elaborate embellishment to create playful and quirky silhouettes.

Advised by:
Della Swain
Course Leader

Graduation/Awards:
Exhibited at London Graduate Fashion Week University Catwalk June 2011
Final major project outfit featured on ITV's "This Morning" June 2011
Final major project outfit featured in the *Daily Express* May 2011
Shortlisted for the Fashion Awareness Direct Competition December 2010
Graduate Fashion Week River Island Recycling Competition Winner June 2009

Mint green silk fuji, patent leather and pleated netting dress with three dimensional chest pieces. White plastic dinosaurs carved by hand then formed into plastic, attached onto the dress with magnets. *Photography by Catwalking.com*

:: Sweatshirt jumper appliqued with latex, plastic, silk velvet devore, glitter organza, lilac, pink and mint green leather, also with riveted stainless steel laser cut geometric shapes. Organza trousers with glitter stencilling. White plastic dinosaur bra carved by hand then formed in plastic, with lilac silk jersey loops. *Photography by Catwalking.com*

:: Oversized sports jacket made from yellow silk jersey with glitter organza, latex, plastic, knit, glitter jersey, and silk chiffon used to embellish the jacket with over the top frills. Mirrored stainless steel laser cut shapes have been riveted on top of the frill embellishment. The skirt is made from loops of silk and cotton jersey, and yellow pleated tulle. *Photography by Catwalking.com*

:: Unitard with exaggerated frill embellishment and three dimensional, laser cut metal star ornamentation. The unitard is made from pink jersey layered with silver metallic knit, embellished with latex, plastic, chiffon, organza, and silk jersey.

:: Three dimensional shooting star top, a star has been pattern cut into a silk crepe and chiffon top with silk pleats falling from the star. The shorts are made from pink wool.

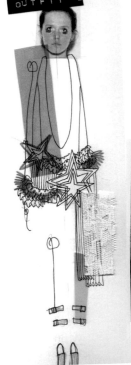

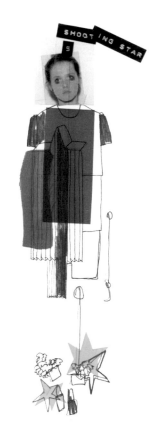

SHIVANI CHAVDA

BA (Hons)
Fashion Design
De Montfort University
Home town/Country:
London, England

Womenswear design

Inspiration:
The inspiration behind my collection was wild animals and surreal art. I created detailed illustrations of the animals and merged them with fluid dream-like paintings, transforming them into fantastical creatures that are not always what they seem. An elegant, but modern collection fully styled with bespoke handmade feather accessories.

Graduation/Awards:
Winner of Clothes Show Live "Young Designer of the Year" Award 2010.
Winner of the BFC Warehouse design competition.
Finalist of the Zandra Rhodes catwalk textiles award at GFW 2011.

Advised by:
Della Swain,
Programme leader
BA hons fashion

Mix media. Watercolor, fine liner, acetate.
Illustration by Shivani Chavda

:: Mix media. Watercolor, fine liner, acetate. *Illustration by Shivani Chavda*

:: Full length silk animal printed dress in rainbow colors. Styled with bespoke feather neckpiece. *Photography by Shivani Chavda*

:: Full length hand illustrated jersey animal printed shift dress. Feather necklace. *Photography by Shivani Chavda*

:: Two piece. Pleated Chiffon animal print trousers with a cropped Jersey symmetrical print top. *Photography by Shivani Chavda*

SARIKA PANCHOLI

BA (Hons)
Fashion Design
De Montfort University
Home town/Country:
Leicester, United
Kingdom

Fashion Design:
Womenswear
specialized in
knitwear

Inspiration:
The collection was
an interpretation
of the culture I have
been surrounded by,
combining vibrant
colors from the Hindu
festival of "Holi" with
traditional British knitwear
techniques.
Using household items,
such as shoelaces,
lollipop sticks, and curtain
rings to embellish with,
on top of the knitwear,
to create extravagant
pieces.

Graduation/Awards:
£2,000 Bursary
   awarded from The
   Worshipful Church of
   Framework Knitters.
At graduate fashion
   week 2011, I was
   awarded the David
   Band textile award at
   the gala ceremony.

Advised by:
Della Swain,
programme leader
BA Hons Fashion

Jersey macramé, with hand knitted traditional
Aran jumper and wool jersey jogging bottoms.
Photography by Catwalking.com

:: Machine knitted multicolored cape, with a cream dress embellished with shoe laces. *Photography by Catwalking.com*

:: Leather t-shirt with shoelace embellishment, and machine knitted jogging bottoms, accessorized with jersey macramé bag. *Photography by Catwalking.com*

:: Dress with vintage cross stitch work, alongside shoelace and bangle embellishment, accessorized with leather clutch. *Photography by Catwalking.com*

:: Crop Aran hand knit jumper, orange embellished vest, with wool jersey jogging bottoms with large pen pockets. *Photography by Catwalking.com*

LAUREN PHAROAH

**BA Honors
Fashion Design
De Montfort University**
Home town/Country:
Coventry, United
Kingdom

**Womenswear
Designer**

Inspiration:
The "Four and Twenty Black Birds," beautifully damaged collection is inspired by the mood between feminine innocence and the female alter ego. The soft and the harsh. The light and the dark. The tender and the rocker. Further inspired by Gothic architecture, rock and biker influences, and sullen photography.

Advised by:
Miss Della Swain

Black origin assured fox fur shrug. Distressed grey and off white under-side leather strapped blazer. Grey and white knit printed silk shirt with silver metal collar tips. Midnight blue glass beaded trousers.

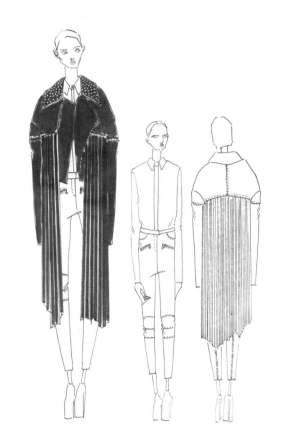

:: Black origin assured fox fur shrug. Distressed grey and off white under-side leather strapped blazer. Grey and white knit printed silk shirt with silver metal collar tips. Midnight blue glass beaded trousers. *Photography by Christopher Moore Limited (catwalking.com)*

:: Black fringed leather oversized biker jacket with studded collar. White glass beaded shirt. White leather trousers with metal zip pockets and zip detail down the back leg to add in fullness to trouser leg.

:: Black fringed leather oversized biker jacket with studded collar. White glass beaded shirt. White leather trousers with metal zip pockets and zip detail down the back leg to add in fullness to trouser leg. *Photography by Christopher Moore Limited (catwalking.com)*

:: Black oversized leather biker jacket with quilted shoulders, in seam fur detail, double belt, and black origin assured fox fur hem. *Photography by Christopher Moore Limited (catwalking.com)*

UME-ROMAAN SACRANIE

BA HONS
Fashion Design
De Montfort University
Home town/Country:
Leicestershire, England

Womenswear

Inspiration:
Inspired by dark, ethereal moods and tones. The collection was predominantly inspired by heavy metals and vintage jewelry. It was a collaboration between the dark and innocence inspired by a melancholic and euphoric color palette. Heavy embellishments and rustic chains are some of the various components inspiring the pieces.

Graduation/Awards:
2010 Young Textile
    Designer Award
Finalist Graduate
    Fashion Week Gold
    Award
Runner Up BFC
    Warehouse
    Competition
Semi Finalist BFC
    Harrods Competition

Advised by:
Della Swain
Programme Leader
BA HONS Fashion

Linked leather dress with metal stones infused into leather linked by metal O-rings. *Photography by Catwalking.com*

:: Beaded fringed leather biker jacket with belts worn with beaded leather skirt textured with thin metal rings. *Photography by Catwalking.com*

:: Embroidered Gothic patterned leather coat, encrusted with beaded stones and embellishments, finished with hand stitched coque bird feathers. Outfit worn with embroidered leather leggings and stitched with metal beads. *Photography by Catwalking.com*

:: Chain fringed leather T-shirt with long fringed chain top worn on top. Outfit worn with beaded leather leggings. *Photography by Catwalking.com*

:: Long chain dress, made with metal chains formed by small and large O-rings. *Photography by Catwalking.com*

HANNAH CUMMING

**BA (Hons)
Fashion Design
Edinburgh College
of Art**
Home town/Country:
Edinburgh, Scotland

Fashion Womenswear

Inspiration:
Personal travels in South
Africa have inspired
me, whilst my research
revisits the glamorous
and eclectic days of
travel. I have a strong
passion for color and
classic, sophisticated
cutting. I design with
the aspiration to make
women feel beautiful
and confident.

Graduation/Awards:
To proceed to study
  MA in Fashion
  Womenswear
  at Edinburgh
  College of Art
Medusa Award 2011
  for best use of color
  and cutting

Advised by:
Mal Burkinshaw,
Programme Director
of Fashion, Edinburgh
College of Art

Silk dress and leather details. Wooden handmade accessory.
Photography by Mitchell Sams

:: Silk dress and
leather details.
Wooden handmade
accessory.
*Photography by
Mitchell Sams*

:: Pencil and inks.
*Illustration by
Hannah Cumming*

:: Pencil and inks.
*Illustration by
Hannah Cumming*

:: Pencil and inks.
*Illustration by
Hannah Cumming*

KYLE GRAHAM SPIRES

BA (Hons)
Fashion Design
Edinburgh College
of Art
Home town/Country:
Edinburgh, Scotland

Fashion Womenswear
and Accessories

Inspiration:
My work is influenced
by the relationship
between cloth and body,
while experimenting
with research into
seduction, movement,
and performance
sportswear. My work
tends to showcase
large flowing forms
juxtaposed with harsh
linear contemporary
tailoring. Within each
outfit, a sense of contrast
often is vital to the overall
aesthetic.

Graduation/Awards:
Winner of Graduate
Fashion Week Karen
Millen Fashion Portfolio
of the year 2011.

Advised by:
Mal Burkinshaw,
Programme Director
Fashion, Edinburgh
College of Art

Leather and silk dress. *Photography by Mitchell Sams*

:: Laser etched leather top, silk pleated trousers. *Photography by Mitchell Sams*

:::: Pencil and inks. *Illustration by Kyle Graham Spires*

KYLE GRAHAM SPIRES

additional panelling to break up solid colour.9

brass plated buckle with double varnish layer.

Pencil, pen, and inks. *Illustration by Kyle Graham Spires*

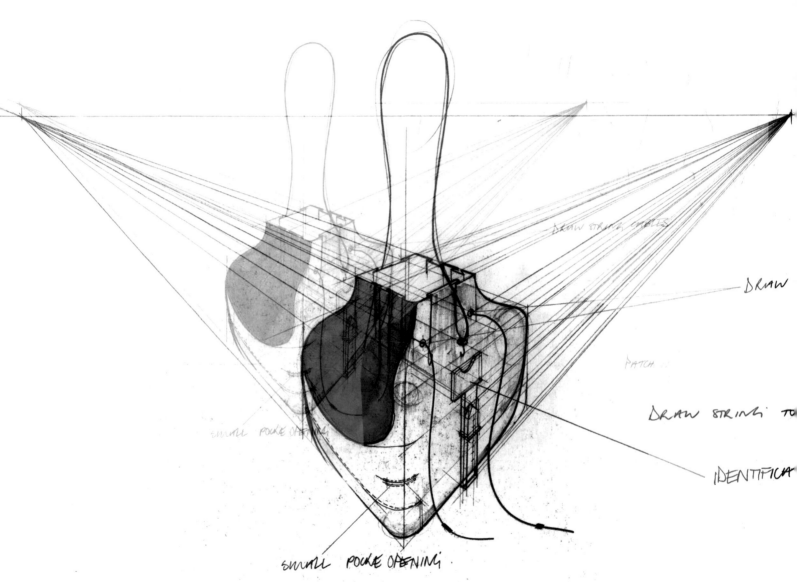

DRAW

PATCH

DRAW STRING TO

IDENTIFICA

SMALL POCKE OPENING.

accessory design and development...

developing a industrialised, multifuctional bag for day + evening wear.

Pencil, pen, and inks. *Illustration by Kyle Graham Spires*

ANIKA HÖPPEL

**BA (Hons)
Fashion Design
Edinburgh College
of Art**
Home town/Country:
Bad Staffelstein,
Germany

**Womenswear
and Knitwear**

Inspiration:
My graduate collection
is based around the
idea of questioning our
need for functionality.
I focused on elements
such as the signifiers of
functionality in active
wear and how these
could be interpreted
in a new way, and if
and how they could be
interpreted in knitwear,
creating a new pseudo-
functionality.

Graduation/Awards:
Achieved First Class
Honors Degree at ECA

Advised by:
Mal Burkinshaw,
Programme Director
of Fashion, Edinburgh
College of Art

Leather dress, knitted top, hand-knit scarf.
Photography by Mitchell Sams

:: Leather dress, knitted top, hand-knit scarf. *Photography by Mitchell Sams*

:: Leather dress, knitted top, leather bag accessories. *Photography by Mitchell Sams*

:: Pencil, guache, and collage mix. *Illustration by Anika Höppel*

:: Pencil, guache, and collage mix. *Illustration by Anika Höppel*

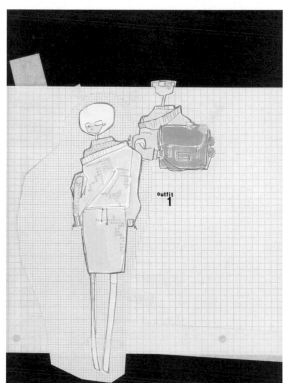

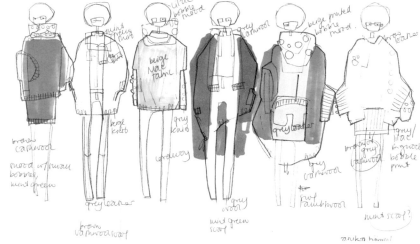

ANNA STEPHENSON

**BA (HONS)
Fashion Design
Edinburgh College
of Art**
Home town/Country:
London, UK

Fashion Womenswear

Inspiration:
My collection illustrates
the strengths and
weaknesses of fabrics
being pulled away and
reconnected; twisted
and manipulated to
their fragile limits. The
collection celebrates
both nature and
modern femininity
through wearable yet
directional cutting.

Graduation/Awards:
I-on Magazine
Graduate of the
Year Award 2011

Advised by:
Mal Burkinshaw,
Programme Director
of Fashion, Edinburgh
College of Art

Digitally printed hand painted floral onto silks,
screen printed flock, and hand cut fabric manipulation.
Photography by Mitchell Sams

:: Digitally printed hand painted floral onto silks, screen printed flock, and hand cut fabric manipulation. *Photography by Mitchell Sams*

:: Digitally printed hand painted floral onto silks, screen printed flock, and hand cut fabric manipulation. *Photography by Mitchell Sams*

:: Pencil, flock, and collage. *Illustration by Anna Stephenson*

:: Pencil, flock, and collage. *Illustration by Anna Stephenson*

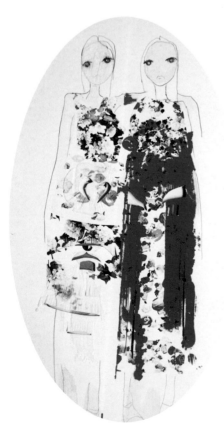

FELIX WOLODYMYR CHABLUK SMITH

BA (HONS)
Fashion Design
Edinburgh College
of Art
Home town/Country:
Edinburgh, Scotland

Fashion Menswear

Inspiration:
Inexorably drawn to the subtleties of menswear, I am ever inspired by the codes, history, and purpose of male dress and fascinated by the semiotics of cut and cloth.

Graduation/Awards:
Graduate Fashion Week Menswear Award 2011
Stuart Parvin Award for Outstanding Studies 2011
Edinburgh College of Art Chairman's Medal 2011
Shortlisted for the GFW Karen Millen Fashion Portfolio Award 2011
British Fashion Council and Burberry Design Competition – Finalist
British Fashion Council Scholarship Winner 2011
Will proceed to study MA Menswear at RCA

Advised by:
Mal Burkinshaw, Programme Director of Fashion, Edinburgh College of Art

Wool suit. *Photography by Mitchell Sams*

:: Leather top, cotton shirt, wool trousers. *Photography by Mitchell Sams*

:: Waterproof coat, cotton shirt, wool trousers. *Photography by Mitchell Sams*

:: Pencil. *Illustration by Felix Wolodymyr Chabluk Smith*

:: Pencil. *Illustration by Felix Wolodymyr Chabluk Smith*

AMBER HUNTER

BA (HONS) Fashion Design for Industry, Heriot-Watt University School of Textiles and Design
Home town/Country: North Berwick, Scotland

Menswear Fashion, Tailoring and Knitwear

Inspiration:
With subtle details inspired by armor, "Body Armor" concentrates on clothing as a form of protection, used as a way of expressing a personality while shielding an identity. The final garment (Image 5) is a theory piece, exploring the clashes between British and Muslim youth culture.

Graduation/Awards:
Incorporation of Bonnet Makers and Dyers of Glasgow Prize 2011
Heriot Watt Outstanding Merit Prize 2011

Grey mohair sculpted jacket with purple silk lining and black mohair/cotton slim fit trousers with grey mohair/cotton pleated panels. *Photography by DN ANDERSON*

⠶ Black cashmere/ purple lambswool machine knitted jumper with layered leatherette tabard and grey mohair/ cotton trousers. *Photography by DN ANDERSON*

⠶ Mens black mohair/cotton one-piece with torso patch detailing. *Photography by DN ANDERSON*

⠶ Black cotton fitted dress, leatherette collar and layered armour shoulder detailing and silk lining. *Photography by DN ANDERSON*

⠶ Black jersey burka mini dress with exposing power-net panels. *Photography by DN ANDERSON*

CLAIRE HUNTER

BA Honors Fashion Design for Industry Heriot-Watt University
Home town/Country: Edinburgh, Scotland

BA Honors Fashion Design for Industry

Inspiration:
Inspiration was sourced from "The Vertical City," a framework of proposed and current sky scrapers existing in Dubai. Floor sweeping hems and high necklines optimize length and height, whilst vertical seams collide to propose an angular drop, the geometric structure of modern architecture.

Graduation/Awards:
Emily Chan Memorial Prize for Best Fashion. Design for Industry student 2009-2010. University Prize of Outstanding Merit 2009-2010.

Advised by:
Mark Timmins Course Director, Fashion Design for Industry

Merino suiting wool with black power mesh inserts. Tailoring techniques. *Photography by Ricco Gallery Photography*

:: Merino suiting wool with black power mesh inserts. The juxtaposition of tailoring and stretch garment construction. *Photography by Ricco Gallery Photography*

:: Cashmere pleated hem skirt lined in merino wool, with merino and power mesh tailored shirt *Photography by Ricco Gallery Photography*

:: CDuchess cotton satin dress with low cut V shaped inverted lapel teamed with power mesh leotard including contrast duchess collar and cuffs. *Photography by Ricco Gallery Photography*

DEBORAH MORGAN

BA (HONS) Fashion Design for Industry School of Textiles & Design Henriot-Watt University
Home town/Country: Haddington, Scotland

Womenswear, Fashion

Inspiration:
Six Man Ray paintings hang on the gallery wall. Minimalistic, clean, and symbolic, they represent one idea. At second glance they represent another. Perception contradicts the paintings. Menswear tailoring on a female creates both an androgynous yet masculine aesthetic. My collection is a second glance, a contradictory perception.

Midnight blue wood cape with tweed lining, poplin shirt dress layered with a knitted white jumper dress.

:: Double collared, optic white poplin cotton shirt dress.

:: Asymmetrical optic white poplin shirt dress with repeated collars and plackets.

:: Optic white poplin shirt with multiple collars and tweed trousers.

:: Midnight blue striped wool trench coat/cloak, inside seams bound in tweed. Detachable cape with inverted tweed box pleat.

LUCY HAUGH

BA (Hons) Fashion
Kingston University
Home town/Country:
Yeovil, Somerset, UK

**Menswear
and Knitwear**

Inspiration:
A growing trend of a reliance on health supplements and enhanced products has inspired this collection. The notion of "fortification" in its widest sense has prompted and inspired the designs, as well as the colors and textures of pill packaging.

Graduation/Awards:
First class
honors degree.

Advised by:
Elinor Renfrew
and Andrew Ibi

Cotton caped parka and knitted high neck jumper.

:: Illustration of cotton caped parka outfit.

:: Knitted mercerised cotton high neck jumper, using ripple knit technique.

:: Illustration of grey suit and red cape.

:: Grey Worsted Wool suit with waterproof cape in Red Schoeller fabric.

LAUREN SANINS

**BA (HONS) Fashion
Kingston University**
Home town/Country:
London, United
Kingdom

Fashion Design:
Womenswear Knit

Inspiration:
Inspired by the graphic symbols created by packaging and mule ties and the wrapped sculptures of Cristo, I wanted garments to look packaged to the wearer. This was achieved through new knit techniques, graphics, and creating a twist on the traditional drawstring, for an elevated casual feel.

Graduation/Awards:
Finalist (1 of 8) to take part in Max Mara's young designer showroom in Reggio Emilia, Italy.
Finalist BFC Warehouse competition 2011, one of eight, showcasing my collection to a panel of industry members.
Finalist (internal) BFC Burberry competition, designing a range of outerwear based on war artist William Orpen.
Finalist for Brooks Brothers competition, designing a new, younger range.

Winner, Banana Republic, designing and making a transitional piece that could be worn for evening, day, and work. Won a 2-month internship at design offices, New York.
Winner, John Smedley knitwear project, designing a capsule collection for a traditional and heritage brand. Won a short placement, based in the Derbyshire mill.
Selected by *Vogue Italia* to have a potential feature on my work.

Advised by:
Elinor Renfrew,
Course Director
Kingston University
Fashion BA (HONS)

Distressed metallic lamb nappa bomber jacket, worn with graphic, silk double fabric knitted dress. *Photography by Lauren Sanins/Omar Fahmi (www.omarfahmi.com)*

Double bonded jersey jacket, with bespoke rope and steel toggle detailing, worn with coated cotton trousers and cotton shirt. *Photography by Lauren Sanins/Omar Fahmi (www.omarfahmi.com)*

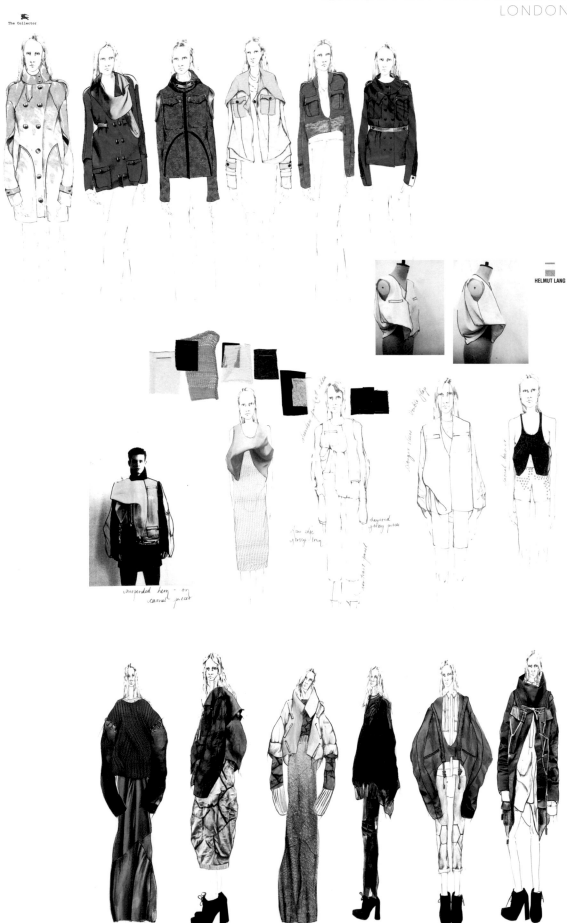

The Collector

HELMUT LANG

::: Line up of Burberry outerwear, based around the idea of embellishment and "waterproof sequins" using coated cottons, silicon, and suede. *Photography by Lauren Sanins*

::: Design development of Helmut Lang knit and outerwear, in cotton and silk yarns and distressed leather. *Photography by Lauren Sanins*

::: Final collection, key fabrics including oil tech cotton, textured silk jersey, and double bonded jersey, including hand knit and leather combinations, shima knit sweaters and rope made from traditional techniques. *Photography by Lauren Sanins*

LAUREN SANINS
COLLECTION 2011

LAURA HELEN SEARLE

BA (Hons) Fashion
Kingston University
Home town/Country:
London, England

Fashion Design:
Womenswear/
Knitwear/Outerwear

Inspiration:
Propaganda: A false scene is set against oppressed tradition— where the old life and military rule struggle to mix. Acidic florals, color, and embroidery overpower a new landscape of flat, worn texture. Dealing with perception and trying to create a collection of contrasts—marrying modern, abstract silhouettes with military nostalgia.

Graduation/Awards:
Commended in Hand
  & Lock Embroidery
  Prize 2011
Student of the Year
  2011 (Kingston
  University)
Portfolio chosen
  for Vogue (*Italia*)
  Talent Event, Milan,
  September 2011

Advised by:
Elinor Renfrew
Fashion Course
Director

Shirt: Washed silk twill/cashmere & merino suiting/neoprene.
Trousers: Cashmere & merino twill suiting.

⠿ Coat: Boiled twill suiting wool with waxed cotton. Knit dress: Pure Scottish cashmere with hand embroidery.

⠿ Coat: Boiled twill suiting wool with waxed cotton. Knit dress: Pure Scottish cashmere with hand embroidery. *Photography by Vincent Dolman, Eline from Select Model Management.*

⠿ Mercerised cotton oversized jumper with hand embossed leather shoulder patches & pure Scottish cashmere knitted dress. Mercerised cotton jumper with hand embroidered patches & cashmere merino twill suiting skirt. *Photography by Vincent Dolman, Eline from Select Model Management*

⠿ Final collection development board: Draping and styling experimentation.

Tinker Tailor Soldier Spy

Laura Helen Searle

Final Collection 2011

SOPHIE LASSEN

**Fashion Design
Kolding School
of Design**
Home town/Country:
Aarhus, Denmark

Fashion Design

Inspiration:
For my menswear collection No.010111, I've been inspired by mugshots of male criminals from the 1930s. I've mostly used the pictures as inspiration for the mood of my collection. I've also been inspired by the theory of the golden ratio, and used it to find marks on the male body, from which I've developed the shape and cut of the collection.

Advised by:
Ulla Ræbild,
Course Coordinator /
Fashion Design

Shirt: woven cotton; pants: wool.
Photographer: Peter Ravnsborg

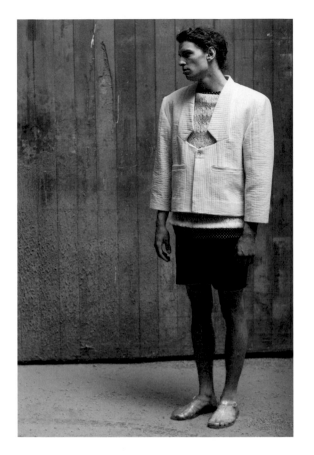

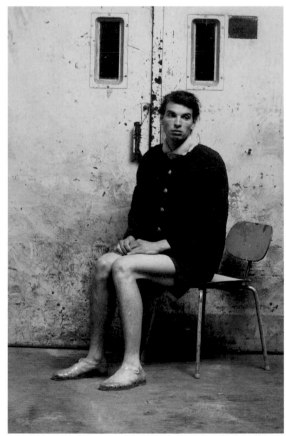

:: Shirt: knitted wool; jacket: quilted cotton, pants: quilted corduroy. *Photographer: Peter Ravnsborg*

:: Shirt: wool; pants: woven cotton. *Photographer: Peter Ravnsborg*

:: Shirt: knitted wool; pants: cotton. *Photographer: Peter Ravnsborg*

:: Jacket: quilted wool; pants: coated cotton. *Photographer: Peter Ravnsborg*

SIFF PRISTED NIELSEN

**Textile Design
Kolding School
of Design**
Home town/Country:
Copenhagen,
Denmark

**Textile Design,
Mixed Media**

Inspiration:
THE GREATEST
SHOW ON EARTH
—is the wonders of nature
and what it creates. I
found my inspiration in
the travelling freak shows
of the late 1800s.
I see the beauty in the
small differences of the
human body and want
the world to embrace
the surprises of nature.

Graduation/Awards:
Grant from Danmarks
Nationalbanks
Jubilæumsfond

Corsage: Branding in natural leather.
Bodystocking: Padding and piping.
Photographer Noam Griegst

:: Bodysuit: Digital knit, wool, and lycra. Hat: Knotting, nylon, and wire. *Photographer Noam Griegst*

:: Fake fur: Hand-knit, nylon tulle. Bodysuit: Digital knit, wool, and lycra. *Photographer Noam Griegst*

:: Shirt: Digital print on corduroy with hand-knitted details. Shorts: Discharge print on cotton. *Photographer Noam Griegst*

:: Backstage photo from the graduation show during Copenhagen Fashion Week SS2012. An overview of my final collection. *Photographer Georg Petermichl*

MARIA PARSONS

**Fashion Design
Kolding School
of Design**
Home town/
Country: Coventry, UK;
Sønderborg, Denmark

**Conceptual/
Avant-garde Fashion**

Inspiration:
The graduation collection is called "BACK TO MYSTERY CITY" and is inspired by the decoration/illustration on a metal tray. In the design process I chose to work directly with the colors and geometric shapes of the illustration, which meant that the final collection turned out very conceptual.
I have incorporated different techniques such as embroidery, quilting, appliqué technique, and beading in my collection.
All of this has been made possible by a production trip to New Delhi, India, in March 2011. The result is a joyous, colorful, and expressive avant-garde fashion collection.

Graduation/Awards:
1st runner up at The Designers' Nest show (February 2009)

Advised by:
Ulla Ræbild,
Course Coordinator /
Fashion Design

Mixed materials; satins, cotton, silk/cotton blend, chiffons.
*Photographer: Rikke Kjær, Collage: Anna Maria Helgadottir,
Model: Emilie R./Scoop Models*

:: Applique technique; satin, silk, polyester, gold lame. *Photographer: Rikke Kjaer, Collage: Anna Maria Helgadottir, Model: Emilie R./ Scoop Models*

:: Beading technique; metallic coating on fake suede/polyester. Beads in different sizes and colors. *Photographer: Rikke Kjaer, Collage: Anna Maria Helgadottir, Model: Emilie R./ Scoop Models*

:: Quilting technique; satin, polyester, crushed velvet, silks, metallic polyester, cottons. *Photographer: Rikke Kjaer, Model: Katinka/ Scoop Models*

:: Pencil on paper, crayons, markers. *Illustration by Maria Parsons*

LOUISE SIGVARDT

**Fashion Design
Kolding School
of Design**
Home town/Country:
Copenhagen,
Denmark

Fashion Design:
Womenswear

Inspiration:
Old new – New old
The project is based on
the transition from "old
luxury" to "new luxury"
in which definitions of
luxury and trends have
been dissolved and
where not only one kind
of luxury applies. The
collection is inspired by
a mixture of the two kinds
of luxury, classic simple
cuts combined with new
materials, compositions,
and details.

Advised by:
Ulla Ræbild,
Course Coordinator,
Fashion Design

Silk velvet and neoprene—evening dress.
*Photo: Sacha Maric, Make-up: Louise Polano,
Model: Ida W/Scoop Models*

:: Silk and neoprene.
Photo: Sacha Maric,
Make-up: Louise
Polano, Model: Ida
W/Scoop Models

:: Silk, wool, wool fixed
on neoprene hand-
dyed silk, denim, and
mohair. Photo: Sacha
Maric, Make-up:
Louise Polano, Model:
Ida W/Scoop Models

:: Silk, wool, wool
fixed on neoprene,
denim, and silk velvet.
Photo: Sacha Maric,
Make-up: Louise
Polano, Model: Ida W/
Scoop Models

:: Illustration of
the second photo
on this page
(silk and neoprene).

AGLA STEFÁNSDÓTTIR

**Fashion Design
Kolding School
of Design**
Home town/Country:
Fljótsdalshérað, Iceland

Fashion Design

Inspiration:
Geometric shapes
are visually dominant
in the collection, but
in folds and cuts they
disappear as suddenly
as they appear. The
movement of the
body underlines this
quality and resembles
a kaleidoscope image,
where the body slides
in and out of the cut
garment, joining and
disjointing it.

Advised by:
Ulla Ræbild,
Course Coordinator /
Fashion Design

Multiple layers of silk, viscose and cotton cut with scissors.
Photography by Evelin Saul

:: Multiple layers of sandwashed silk, organdy and cotton cut with scissors. *Photography by Evelin Saul*

:: Multiple layers of grograin silk, viscose and linen cut with scissors. *Photography by Glamour • The Concept Boutique*

:: Multiple layers of silk, viscose and cotton cut with scissors. *Photography by Glamour • The Concept Boutique*

:: Jacket: quilted wool; pants: coated cotton. *Photographer: Peter Ravnsborg*

MARK DEMPSEY

**BA in Fashion Design
Limerick School
of Art and Design**
Home town/Country:
Offaly, Ireland

Inspiration:
Based on the 1988 manga movie entitled *Akira*. The complex and layered relationship between the main characters inspired a collection focused on the practices of Japanese pattern cutting techniques, couture, and sportswear.

Advised by:
Anne Melinn

Top and trousers incorporating innovative cutting and stand work in mercerised cotton, cotton canvas, and leather.

:: Top incorporating innovative cutting and stand work in mercerised cotton and cotton canvas with silk jersey leggings.

:: Dress incorporating innovative cutting and stand work in silk jersey and leather.

:: Photoshop and Illustrator.

:: Photoshop and Illustrator.

KARLY HODGE

BA in Fashion Design
Limerick School
of Art and Design
Home town/Country:
Clare, Ireland

Inspiration:
Inspired by the energy
and chaos of New York
City, and the structural
elements of the cityscape
and subway system.

Graduation/Awards:
Award for best
use of fabric in a
graduate collection.

Advised by:
Anne Melinn

100% wool double faced jacquard knit jacket created on
Shima Seiki technology. Denim and neoprene jeans.

:: Plastic and PVC dress with denim and leather strip

:: Stretch PVC top and denim jeans with PVC piping.

:: Photoshop and Illustrator

:: Photoshop

Karly Hodge
9am on the New York Subway

9am On The New York Subway

SINEAD LEONARD

**BA in Fashion Design
Limerick School
of Art and Design**
Home town/Country:
Waterford, Ireland

Inspiration:
Inspired by the childhood
ritual of finding a quiet,
hidden place from the
world to rekindle spirit
and creativity, where
sparkling ideas would
come to life.

Advised by:
Anne Melinn

Recycled pieces incorporating draped cotton mix with lace
insert and fur collar embellished with beading and trinkets.

:: Recycled pieces incorporating pleated and gathered chiffon with tulle, embellished with beading, trinkets, and chiffon rosettes.

:: Recycled pieces incorporating pleated cotton mix with lace, embellished with beading, trinkets, and fur.

:: Photoshop and Illustrator.

:: Photoshop and Illustrator.

WATCH WITH GLITTERING EYES
THE WHOLE WORLD AROUND YOU
BECAUSE THE GREATEST SECRETS
ARE ALWAYS HIDDEN IN THE MOST UNLIKELY PLACES

SINEAD LEONARD
ILLUSTRATION BOARD

SINEAD LEONARD

JANE MCKENNA

BA in Fashion Design
Limerick School
of Art and Design
Home town/Country:
Offaly, Ireland

Inspiration:
Inspired by the *Coppelia*
ballet, which is about a
doll maker who is trying
to breathe life into a doll
whom he loves. Also
inspired by clown dolls
collected as a child.

Graduation/Awards:
Winner of the "AIB
Business Development
Award"—Awarded
to the best graduate
collection.

Advised by:
Anne Melinn

Cotton and tulle dress. Layering and applique
with yarn dolls attached.

:: Jacquard knit dress in cotton blends with fringing.

:: Cotton and tulle dress. Layering and applique with yarn dolls attached.

:: Photoshop

:: Photoshop

JANE MCKENNA
TOYING WITH REALITY
GARMENT NO 3 - JACKET, SKIRT & SHORTS
AUTUMN/ WINTER

JANE MCKENNA
TOYING WITH REALITY
MOOD BOARD

AOIDIN SAMMON

**BA in Fashion Design
Limerick School of
Art and Design**
Home town/Country:
Kildare, Ireland

Inspiration:
Influenced by
architectural and
engineering concepts,
particularly the evolution
of the beauty and
skill of hand crafted
techniques and the
finesse of technological
developments.

Advised by:
Anne Melinn

Rubber and organza dress

AOIDÍN SAMMON

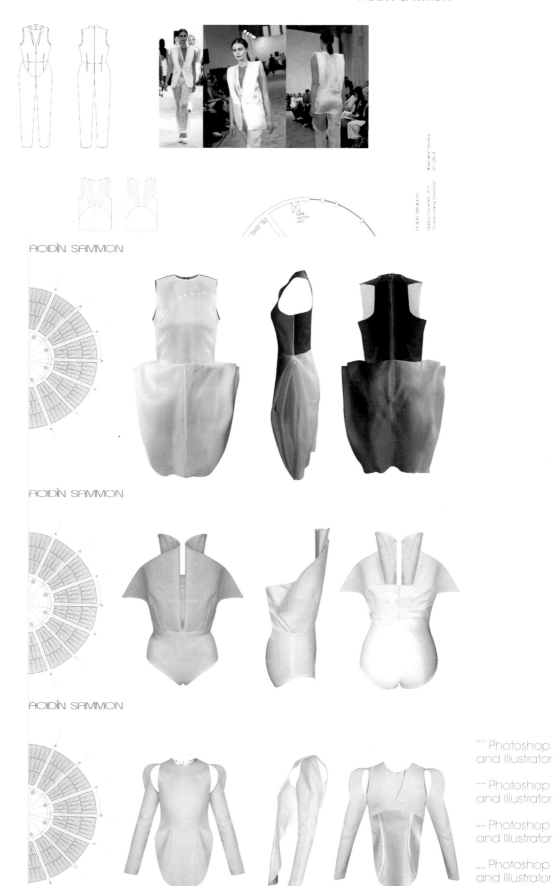

AOIDÍN SAMMON

AOIDÍN SAMMON

AOIDÍN SAMMON

.... Photoshop
and Illustrator

.... Photoshop
and Illustrator

.... Photoshop
and Illustrator

.... Photoshop
and Illustrator

ANGELA BRANDYS

**BA (Hons) Fashion
Design Technology:
Womenswear
London College
of Fashion**
Home town/Country:
Great Britain

Womenswear

Inspiration:
This collection does not favor the superficial façade presented by the mass media dictatorship currently in play. It explores a more "real" tension of new fabric, texture, and color arrangements focusing on ones ability to create in a personal way without rule or order. The designer is drawn to tactile, textured, cleverly colorful elements that she uses as ingredients to design with. This Spring Summer/12 collection fuses many inspirations but predominate emerging references are—1950s nostalgic home dress making, customization, viper girl burlesque excess, decoration, and a vision of an abundance of clashing, dancing, empowered women who can dress for themselves and do it themselves. However, in short, these are clothes the designer has made for herself to wear out. Textiles, textures, fabrics, colors, and decoration are found from all over, and purposefully (often symmetrically) placed across outfits to create an excessive, dramatic, sexy look.
All the ingredients (of which there are masses) are intentionally cheap and layered together to create a new richness. This is all about having fun and doing it for you!

Advised by:
Rob Phillips.
Creative Director,
School of Design &
Technology, London
College of Fashion

Bricolage of materials, trims, and finishings.
Photography by James Finnigan

:: Bricolage of
materials, trims,
and finishings.
*Photography by
James Finnigan*

:: Bricolage of
materials, trims,
and finishings.
*Photography by
James Finnigan*

:: Bricolage of
materials, trims,
and finishings.
*Photography by
James Finnigan*

:: Bricolage of
materials, trims,
and finishings.
*Photography by
James Finnigan*

LIEN BUI

BA (Hons) Fashion Design Technology: Womenswear London College of Fashion

Home town/Country:
Vietnam – Poland
(Vietnamese Polish)

Womenswear

Inspiration:
Work Crash
The main inspirations behind this collection are the qualities of Tamara de Lempicka's paintings, the frame of streamlined automobiles, and the bold mixture of texture and color of Nikolai Howalt's photographic studies on car crashes. The project crosses European Art Deco aesthetics with American Art Deco movements that are inspired by the machine age. Each outfit is created through forward thinking and innovative pattern cutting techniques. Every cutting/sewing line is defined through a clever and tactile usage of different colors, textures, and fabrics all carefully selected and purposefully placed to highlight the contouring definitions of the silhouette. The result is a collection of high impact graphic pieces full of modern vibrancy.

Advised by:
Rob Phillips.
Creative Director,
School of Design &
Technology, London
College of Fashion

Mixed Material—From wool, coated cottons, fleeces to plastic weaves, individually shaped and cut sequins, etc.
Photography by Sean Michael

:: Mixed Material—
From wool, coated
cottons, fleeces
to plastic weaves,
individually shaped
and cut sequins, etc.
*Photography by
Sean Michael*

:: Mixed Material—
From wool, coated
cottons, fleeces
to plastic weaves,
individually shaped
and cut sequins, etc.
*Photography by
Sean Michael*

:: Mixed Material—
From wool, coated
cottons, fleeces
to plastic weaves,
individually shaped
and cut sequins, etc.
*Photography by
Sean Michael*

:: Mixed Material—
From wool, coated
cottons, fleeces
to plastic weaves,
individually shaped
and cut sequins, etc.
*Photography by
Sean Michael*

JOHANNA PIHL

BA (Hons) Fashion Design Technology: Womenswear London College of Fashion

Home town/Country: Sweden

Womenswear

Inspiration:

The Collection was built on an investigation into the relationship between the body's anatomy and the fascination with genetic enhancement through surgery, focusing research on the juxtaposition of our natural form with the cold metals of machinery. By using trapunto techniques the garments demonstrate that our anatomy is engineered and calculated like an engine, showing that by altering and reorganizing our appearance through plastic surgery we diminish our human design. The idea of veins within our bodies, led the research into roads and pipes used in the modern world, and how they function in a carefully calculated way. This idea of nature against synthetic is a recurring theme. The pattern pieces themselves (obviously) became an integral element to the symbolism of what is manmade. The patterns show the graphic, linear, symmetrical perfection that many strive for via surgical enhancement. The pattern pieces became a body map of illustrations depicting new, vein-like forms. They not only show how to manufacture a garment, but via the craft method of trapunto, over time, each curve and line becomes continually followed, used, and starts to diminish, looking old and worn down as any form naturally will age.

Graduation/Awards:

Young fashion industry
   award 2011: Winner
Barnet Lawson trimming
   prize 2011: Finalist
The English National Ballet, the Ballet
   Russes 2010 march: Winner

Advised by:

Rob Phillips.
Creative Director,
School of Design &
Technology, London
College of Fashion

Wool Revere coat with hand-shaded leather inserts.
Photography by James Finnigan

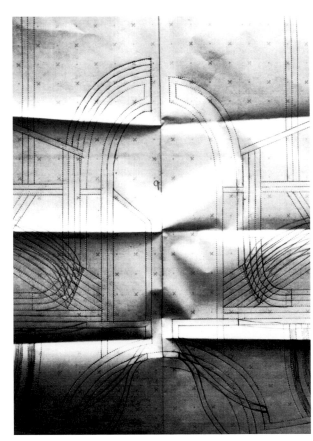

:: Trapunto leather jacket and suede low hung taper cut trousers. *Photography by James Finnigan*

:: Paper & Pen. *Trapunto engineered design pattern piece*

:: Trapunto sample in thick low-stretch jersey. *Trapunto engineered design sample*

:: Pen.

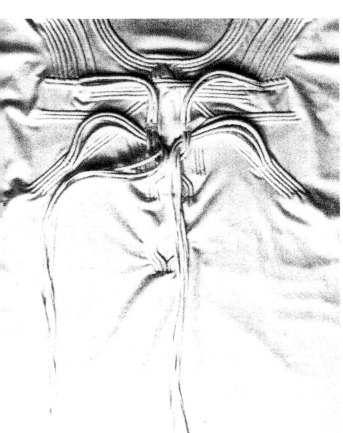

NATALIE RAE

**BA (Hons) Fashion Design Technology: Womenswear
London College of Fashion**
Home town/Country:
United States of America

Womenswear

Inspiration:

This debut collection fuses bold embroidery and a natural color palette with casual American 1980s silhouettes. Inspired by the anthropomorphic artwork of artist Ryan Berkeley, each of the six looks invokes the spirit of well-shod wildlife from Berkeley's animal portraiture. Using a different animal from six of Berkeley's illustrations, Natalie has brought together elements of nature photography, detail from Victorian period animal illustrations as well as experimental painting techniques. The collection balances organic, ethically sourced fabrics and material with a fashion forward sensibility. Fabrics for this collection come from organics suppliers in India and the UK. The majority of this collection's fabrics have been hand-dyed to match the warm palette of Berkeley's illustrations. The one-of-a-kind engineered embroidery work was designed by Natalie Rae and crafted by Hand and Lock of London.

Graduation/Awards:

Shortlisted for WGSN 2010 Global
  Fashion Awards for Most Creative
  Student Collection
Shortlisted for Wolf and Badger 2010
  Graduate Design Awards
Featured in Italian *Vogue* September
  2010 sublet New Design Talents

Advised by:

Rob Phillips.
Creative Director,
School of Design &
Technology, London
College of Fashion

Organic, ethically sourced fabrics and material.
Photography by Sean Michael

:: Organic, ethically sourced fabrics and material. *Photography by Sean Michael*

:: Organic, ethically sourced fabrics and material. *Photography by Sean Michael*

:: Organic, ethically sourced fabrics and material. *Photography by Sean Michael*

:: Organic, ethically sourced fabrics and material. *Photography by Sean Michael*

KARISHMA SHAHANI

BA (Hons) Fashion Design Technology:
Womenswear
London College of Fashion
Home town/Country: India

Womenswear

Inspiration:
Yatra

My work is a representation of all that inspires me. Three dimensional creations that resonate cultural and social inspirations predominantly form the basis of my influences. Colors, textures, and crafts are three aspects I enjoy exploring. Passions to create and learn new things are factors that drive me toward achieving my goals.

India: The land of dreams and romance, of fabulous wealth and stark scarcity, of splendor and rags, of palaces and hovels, of famine and pestilence, of genie and giants, tigers and elephants, the city, the jungle, of a thousand religions and two million gods, the epitome of legends and traditions. The collection draws inspiration and elements from the multiple layers of India's vibrant culture that continuously creates colorful, vivid, and eclectic experiences for the onlooker. The colors are picked from traditional painting of Indian Gods, and recreated through natural methods of dyeing. In its essence, this collection is a reflection of the Indian lifestyle of re-interpretation of materials and their function at every step, always re-using and recycling, creating heirlooms that are passed down through generations. Each garment is made with beauty, simplicity, and versatility at its core, which lends it a multi-layered and personality driven charm. The designs combine a fusion of two extremes, making the collection experimental and unconventional, while being hinged on modern functionality. This collection gives us a peek in the incredible "Atulya" Indian Experience.

Graduation/Awards:
"Best Surface Textiles 2010" LCF BA Graduate Show
Joint Winner "Nina De York Illustration Award" 2010
"Fashion Graduate of the Year 2010" British
    Graduate 100 Award

Advised by:
Rob Phillips.
Creative Director,
School of Design &
Technology, London
College of Fashion

Multi-material, embroidery techniques, finishes, etc. ranging from cotton to glass incorporating recycled and new elements. *Photography by Sean Michael*

:: Multi-material, embroidery techniques, finishes, etc. ranging from cotton to glass incorporating recycled and new elements. *Photography by Sean Michael*

:: Multi-material, embroidery techniques, finishes, etc. ranging from cotton to glass incorporating recycled and new elements. *Photography by Sean Michael*

:: Multi-material, embroidery techniques, finishes, etc. ranging from cotton to glass incorporating recycled and new elements. *Photography by Sean Michael*

:: Multi-material, embroidery techniques, finishes, etc. ranging from cotton to glass incorporating recycled and new elements. *Photography by Sean Michael*

RACHAEL CAPPER

BA (Hons) Fashion Manchester School of Art
Home town/Country: Stoke on Trent, United Kingdom

Inspiration:
Rachael's strong shapes were inspired by Georgian clothing and men's Victorian shirts held in the archives of the Victoria and Albert Museum in London.

Graduation/Awards:
Rachael was a finalist in the Fashion Awareness Direct competition at London Fashion Week in February 2011.

Advised by:
Alison Welsh, Programme Leader for Fashion at Manchester School of Art

Cotton poplin oversized gathered skirt and cape top, with foam filled gathers. *Photography by Adrian Hunter, Manchester Metropolitan University*

:: Cotton poplin cap-sleeve double-layer collared shirt with gathered waist trousers. *Photography by Adrian Hunter, Manchester Metropolitan University*

:: High-necked gathered cape with pencil trousers. *Photography by Adrian Hunter, Manchester Metropolitan University*

:: Trapeze shape shirt with gathered cotton poplin skirt over circular-cut trousers. *Photography by Adrian Hunter, Manchester Metropolitan University*

:: A-line folded dress with cotton poplin underskirt. *Photography by Adrian Hunter, Manchester Metropolitan University*

JOHN EARNSHAW

**BA (Hons) Fashion
Manchester
School of Art**
Home town/Country:
Stockport,
United Kingdom

Inspiration:
Inspired by photographs
of his grandmother from
the 1950s, John gives
sophisticated garments
a contemporary twist by
mixing classic shapes
with textured fabrics
and crystal embellishment.

Advised by:
Alison Welsh,
Programme Leader for
Fashion at Manchester
School of Art

Foil-printed cropped shirt with crystal-embellished calf-length
skirt. *Photography by Adrian Hunter, Manchester Metropolitan
University*

:: Oversized cotton drill padded jacket teamed with calf-length skirt. *Photography by Adrian Hunter, Manchester Metropolitan University*

:: Metallic foil-printed calf-length skirt with mesh polo neck top and quilted cropped shirt. *Photography by Adrian Hunter, Manchester Metropolitan University*

:: Metallic foil-printed lame gathered skirt with mesh polo neck top and checked silk shirt. *Photography by Adrian Hunter, Manchester Metropolitan University*

:: Foil-printed pleated skirt and mesh shirt with metallic collar detail. *Photography by Adrian Hunter, Manchester Metropolitan University*

OLIVIA HEWITT

**BA (Hons) Fashion
Manchester
School of Art**
Home town/Country:
Heswall, United
Kingdom

Inspiration:
Olivia is inspired by color
and texture, particularly
the innovative use of
print by Michael Angel
and the late Alexander
McQueen.

Advised by:
Alison Welsh,
Programme Leader for
Fashion at Manchester
School of Art

Metal beaded top teamed with digitally printed silk skirt.
*Photography by Adrian Hunter, Manchester Metropolitan
University*

:: Digitally printed stretch cotton dress with racer back. *Photography by Adrian Hunter, Manchester Metropolitan University*

:: Screen printed silk chiffon dress over digitally printed catsuit. *Photography by Adrian Hunter, Manchester Metropolitan University*

:: Digitally printed silk chiffon dress with digitally printed long sleeve top. *Photography by Adrian Hunter, Manchester Metropolitan University*

:: Digitally printed stretch cotton dress with metal bead detail. *Photography by Adrian Hunter, Manchester Metropolitan University*

JOANNA MANDLE

BA (Hons) Fashion Manchester School of Art
Home town/Country: Lichfield, United Kingdom

Inspiration:
Joanna takes inspiration from the childhood adventures she had growing up in the countryside and aims to capture themes of make-believe, fantasy, and nature in her garments.

Graduation/Awards:
Joanna was a finalist in the Fashion Awareness Direct competition at London Fashion Week in February 2011.

Advised by:
Alison Welsh, Programme Leader for Fashion at Manchester School of Art

Oversized pussy-bow shirt with slim fit trousers.
*Photography by Adrian Hunter,
Manchester Metropolitan University*

:: Puff sleeve blouse with laser cut double-layer skirt. *Photography by Adrian Hunter, Manchester Metropolitan University*

:: Metallic frilled cape with bell-embellished collar over silk blouse and plastic layered skirt. *Photography by Adrian Hunter, Manchester Metropolitan University*

:: Long sleeved multi-fabric layered dress. *Photography by Adrian Hunter, Manchester Metropolitan University*

:: Multi-fabric layered dress teamed with velvet jacket and oversized taffeta bow. *Photography by Adrian Hunter, Manchester Metropolitan University*

ESTHER PHILLIPSON

BA (Hons) Fashion Manchester School of Art
Home town/Country: Preston, United Kingdom

Inspiration:
Inspired by color and culture, Esther's bold collection draws from a recent trip to Thailand. She mixes fabrics and texture, digital and screen prints with tribal-inspired Fair Isle patterns.

Graduation/Awards:
A garment from Esther's collection was short-listed for ITV "This Morning Viewers" Award, appearing on national television.

Advised by:
Alison Welsh, Programme Leader for Fashion at Manchester School of Art

Digitally printed drape dress with machine knit poncho edged in Mongolian sheepskin. *Photography by Adrian Hunter, Manchester Metropolitan University*

:: Digitally printed harem pants and machine knit cropped jumper with Mongolian sheepskin trimmed sleeves. *Photography by Adrian Hunter, Manchester Metropolitan University*

:: Digitally printed crepe shirt with Mongolian sheepskin striped skirt and machine knit belt. *Photography by Adrian Hunter, Manchester Metropolitan University*

:: Machine knit tunic with digitally printed snood. *Photography by Adrian Hunter, Manchester Metropolitan University*

:: Digitally printed jumpsuit with Mongolian sheepskin neckpiece. *Photography by Adrian Hunter, Manchester Metropolitan University*

FAH CHAKSHUVEJ

**Fashion
Menswear (MA)
Royal College of Art**
Home town/Country:
Bangkok, Thailand

Menswear

Inspiration:
"Amore Armor" depicts love and disappointment of an impossible romance between a knight and a princess. Extreme, yet subtle and contemporary shapes were inspired by armoury. Tailored to fit but still holding its own silhouette using her own techniques and development in modern tailoring and cuts taking menswear to another level.

Graduation/Awards:
Jul 2011 - Winner of ITS#10 Maison Martin Margiela Award, Italy
Jul 2011 - ITS#10 Fashion Design Award Finalist, Italy
Jun 2011 - Winner of The Conran Foundation Award, London
Jun 2008 - First Prize for the People Tree Ethical Fashion Design Award, London
Aug 2007 – Sep 2007: ONE of 5 students for student exchange programme to India. The Pearl Academy of Fashion, New Delhi. Funded by the British council.

Advised by:
Ike Rust and Professor Wendy Dagworthy

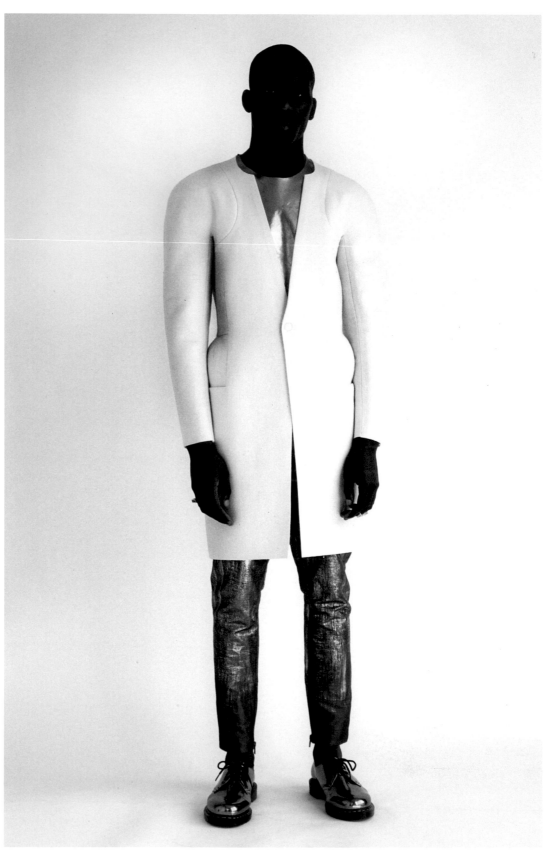

Double wool tailored coat, gold leather vest, gold foil print on denim jeans with tailored calf. *Photo by Christina Smith, Model: Emmanuelle Lawal.*

:: Double wool tailored jacket with minimal seams and maximum silhouette. Foil print on denim pleated jeans. *Photo by Fah Chakshuvej, Model: Emmanuelle Lawal*

:: Bomber jacket with laser etched leather applied with personal burning and painting leather treatments. Detachable laser cut and studded latex cuffs. *Photo by Fah Chakshuvej, Model: Emmanuelle Lawal*

:: Leather and double wool clean-tailored biker jacket. Leather vest. Tailored calf wool trousers with studding details. *Photo by Fah Chakshuvej, Model: Emmanuelle Lawal*

:: Laser cut latex, leather, and metal jewelry (by designer). Metallic leather and double wool tailored coat with side pleats and flat shaping (inner piece). Laser cut+etching on grey rubber coated fabric creating modern man-lace on sweatshirt. *Photo by Fah Chakshuvej, Model: Emmanuelle Lawal*

RUTH GREEN

**MA Fashion
Womenswear
Knitwear
The Royal
College of Art**
Home town/Country:
Bourne, Lincolnshire

**Womenswear
Knitwear**

Inspiration:
Inspiration taken from
the work of Egon Schiele,
colors and textures
melt into one-another.
Combining felted
lambswool, high shine
viscoses, and layers of
sheer silk chiffon, the
collection embodies the
notion of juxtaposition.
Large scale intarsia's
take inspiration from
Francis Giacobetti's
photography cascaded
across oversized
silhouettes, and
slouched lambswool
and mohair intarsia
hand knits.

Graduation/Awards:
ITS 10 competitor—
  Winner of Skunkfunk
  sustainability award
  2011.
Loro Piana Best
  Knitwear Collection
  RCA 2011.
British Fashion Council
  Colleges Council
  and Warehouse
  Competition winner
  2009.

Advised by:
Sarah Dallas.
Head of Fashion
Knitwear—The Royal
College of Art.

Felted lambswool intarsia moulded felt dress with fine gauge fully fashion red Filpucci Viscose. *Photography by Andy Barnham photography- www.andybarnham.com*

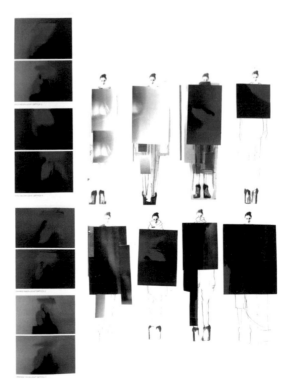

:: Rowan 100% wool chunky hand knit with red fine gauge fully fashioned Filpucci Viscose jumper. Black silk chiffon tailored trouser. *Photography by Andy Barnham photography- www. andybarnham.com*

:: Rowan 100% wool chunky hand knit with red fine gauge fully fashioned Filpucci Viscose jumper. Black silk chiffon tailored trouser. *Photography by Andy Barnham photography- www. andybarnham.com*

:: Rowan 100% wool chunky fisherman's rib snood. Lambswool intarsia felt cape. Fully fashioned Black Filpucci viscose dress. *Photography by Andy Barnham photography- www. andybarnham.com*

:: Ruth Green sketchbook 2011. Francis Giacobetti Photography development. *Illustration by Ruth Green sketchbook 2011*

NICOLA MORGAN

**MA Fashion
Womenswear
Royal
College of Art**
Home town/Country:
London, UK

Womenswear

Inspiration:
A collision between
fashion and jewelry,
Tension Collection
creates gravity-defying
drapes with a powerful
feeling. Skeletal forms
envelop the body,
providing a dynamic
framework from which
flowing evening dresses
are constructed,
combining taut jersey
with soft tailoring to
create strong graphic
contrasts between
fabric and flesh.

Graduation/Awards:
The British Fashion
Council MA
Scholarship

Advised by:
Tristan Webber,
Senior Womenswear
Tutor

Top: Superfine jersey with silver plated rapid prototype.
Photography: Jerome Hunt, Model: Helena @ Union Models

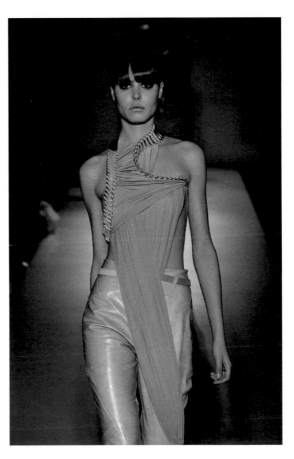

:: Dress: Superfine jersey with enamel finished rapid prototype. *Photography: Jerome Hunt, Model: Helena @ Union Models, Hat: Zara Gorman*

:: Top: Superfine jersey with enamel finished rapid prototype. Trouser: Washed silk. *Photography Chris Moore*

:: Dress: Superfine jersey with enamel finished rapid prototype, leather, and Swarovski trim. *Photography Chris Moore*

:: Top: Superfine jersey with silver plated rapid prototype. Trouser: Italian calf leather. Belt: Baby calfskin. *Photography Chris Moore*

YEJON PARK

**Menswear Fashion
Royal College of Art**
Home town/Country:
Republic of Korea /
Seoul

Menswear Design

Inspiration:
My collection was based on graphic design. The main focus was to successfully merge a 2 dimensional graphic composition with a 3 dimensional structure. So, as the garment falls and folds along the body line, the movement also changes the black and white graphic surface of the garment. The whole idea could be summed up as the correlation between the graphic, shape, and movement.

Graduation/Awards:
2010 June: Umbro
   International Award
2007 Oct: Asian
   Young Fashion
   Designers Contest
   (First Runner up)

Advised by:
Professor Ike Rust,
Professor Peter Siddell

Dancewear inspired collection.

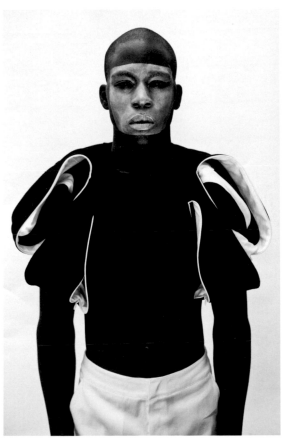

:: RCA graduate collection—Tone changing jacket: Screen print, zip front, variated raglan sleeve.

:: Machine inspired collection: Neoprene, mathematically calculated triangular pieces forming gradually receding spikes down the back.

:: RCA graduate collection—Multi-armhole vest with white zips: Three armholes on each side, which can be zipped up by preference; the shape changes with each hole the wearer puts his arm through.

:: Geometry inspired collection—Dart arm cardigan: Vertical dart on the side arm creating protrusion, micro pleats are bent along the protrusion, creating optical effect.

SASKIA SCHIJEN

**MA Fashion
Womenswear
Royal College of Art**
Home town/Country:
Krefeld, Germany

Womenswear

Inspiration:
The work of Wolfgang
Tillmans, old issues of
The Face and i-D from
the early 1990s, realness,
my friends and their
wardrobes, music,
hipsterdykes, the original
ck One campaign,
Larry Clark's Kids, and
the Dalston Kingsland
shopping center.

Advised by:
Professor Wendy
Dagworthy, Tristan
Webber, David Kappo

Washed white cotton shirt with frayed denim detail on collar
and metal collar bar. *Photography: Elliot Kennedy,
Hair/Make-up: Lauren Murray and Amelia Mullins,
Model: Magdalena Buczek*

:: Viscose knit and nylon rib jersey long sleeve top worn with oversized stone washed denim with painted on stripe at bottom. *Photography: Elliot Kennedy, Hair/ Make-up: Lauren Murray and Amelia Mullins, Model: Magdalena Buczek*

:: Top: Chenille and elastic knit sports underwear worn with oversized stone washed denim with graphic bleach effect, accessorized with long black leather belt with gold and silver plated buckle. *Photography: Elliot Kennedy, Hair/ Make-up: Lauren Murray and Amelia Mullins, Model: Magdalena Buczek*

:: Chenille and elastic knit sports underwear worn with oversized stone washed denim with graphic bleach effect, accessorized with long black leather belt with gold and silver plated buckle.

SASKIA SCHIJEN

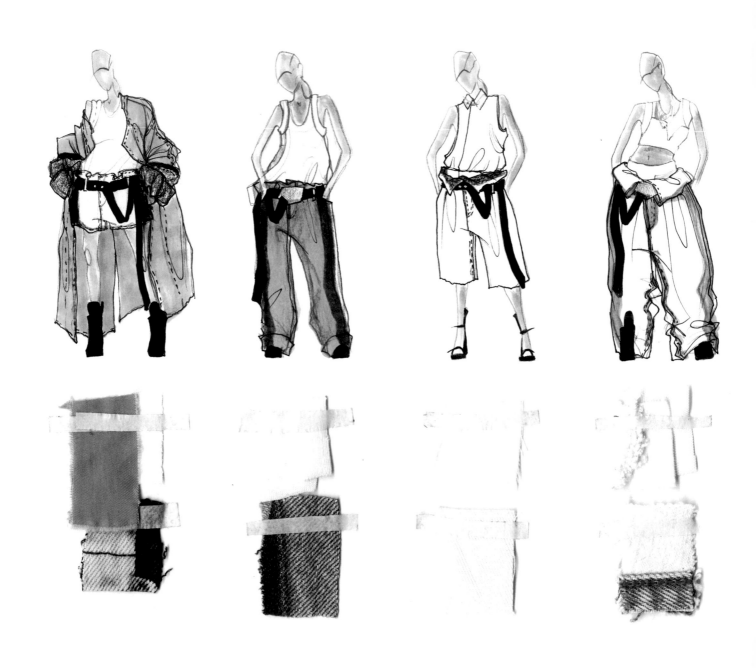

Drawn line-up of the collection with fabric samples; main
materials are denim with graphic wash, bleach, and dye
effects and washed cottons.

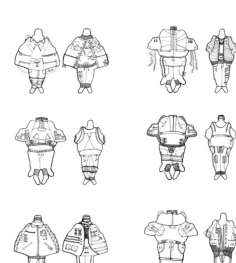

REBECCA FREDERIKSEN

Inspiration:
I always work with the female body as my inspiration and it is my goal with my design to emphasize and substantiate it. It is important in my work to bring color, shape or pattern together in symbiosis. This project was inspired by Art Deco and Diors New Look. It is a contemporary collection with focus on the ornament in the shape.

KAMILLA HOFFMAN

Inspiration:
Inside the Outside

"There is no vision without thought. But to think will not make anyone see. Visual experience is a conditional thought and is created when something happens in the body and so encourages it to think." (Kølvraa 1997)

I have a general interest in classical and functional fashion design, challenging the balance between the feminine and masculine and the recognizable and the unfamiliar.

I challenge perception of shape, texture, and perspective through the relation between a machine knitted pattern and a digitally printed photograph of the knitted pattern.

My inspiration I find in fictional moods and spaces often with references to uniforms and outdoor activities.

MILLA JAMILA NORDLUND

ANNE REMIEN THOMSEN

Inspiration:
The collection mirrors an abandoned house, its decay and the mysterious mood that very often surrounds it. By the absence of residents, an abandoned house is left to decay and disrepair. All the objects of the house formerly controlled and tamed by the human hand now have their own lives. Plants, mold, and moths have worn down, eaten, and overtaken everything as they create uncontrolled motifs, which blur and obstruct the former functions of the interior. Shining surfaces, clean lines, and strong colors are now bleached by the sun, stained by the water, and dusted by the wind. This new, uncontrolled life is mysterious and gives vent to the imagination.

I have applied the interplay between fantasy and reality to my collection for women. In order to achieve this I have used well known materials in new constellations, given decorations their own lives and created contrasts in forms and shapes.

I have worked towards an objective registration of the decay of abandoned houses in the expression, mood, shapes, and composition of my collection.

JAKOB BOESEN

**Fashion Design BA
TEKO**
Home town/Country:
Herning, Denmark

Menswear

Inspiration:
A collection with inspiration drawn from classic menswear. Brought together in clean graphic cuts. A signature style of simple, modern, and carefully designed details.
The design research was done within geological phenomena such as erosion and craters. Also modern and technological ways of observing nature's topography caught my attention. Basically the collection illustrates a "crater."

Graduation/Awards:
Nominated for
    The Golden Fur
    Pin, hosted by
    Kopenhagen Fur.
Nominated for
    Designers Nest.
Accepted for the MA
    Menswear Course at
    Central Saint Martins
    London.

Advised by:
Ingrid Søe,
Head of Design TEKO

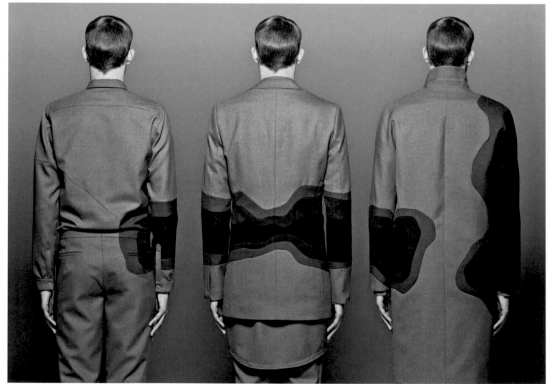

Photographer Mikkel Völcker Petersen

:: *Photographer*
Mikkel Völcker
Petersen

:: *Photographer*
Mikkel Völcker
Petersen

:: *Photographer*
Mikkel Völcker
Petersen

CHRISTIAN HELMER

**Fashion Design BA
TEKO**
Home town/Country:
Aalborg, Denmark

Fashion Design BA

Graduation/Award:
Nominated for
Designers Nest
2007-2011

Photography by Bibi Berge. Photographer. Model: Pernille Moller, Hair: Kristine Bertelsen

:: *Photography by Bibi Berge Photographer, Model Pernille Moller, Hair Kristine Bertelsen*

:: *Photography by Bibi Berge Photographer, Model Pernille Moller, Hair Kristine Bertelsen*

:: *Photography by Bibi Berge Photographer, Model Pernille Moller, Hair Kristine Bertelsen*

:: *Photography by Bibi Berge Photographer, Model Pernille Moller, Hair Kristine Bertelsen*

STEPHANIE KALDHUSSAETTER SIKKES

**Fashion Design
TEKO, Denmark**
Home town/Country:
Oslo, Norway

Fashion Design:
PBA

Inspiration:
The authentic heart, artist Ernesto Neto and architect Zaha Hadid, has inspired me to form a feminine, clean, yet organic and sculptural collection. Key words are biomorphic, fragile, rough, chamber, space, complex, red, floating, closed, powerful, and inner body.
The colletction is called Biomorphic Chamber.

Graduation/Awards:
First runner up in Designers Nest, February 2011, a design competition for 31 Scandinavian students during CPH-fashion week.

Advised by:
Jens Laugesen,
  Designer
Ike Rust,
  Royal College of Art
Birgitta Johansson,
  Head of Design
  at TEKO

Silk blouse in layers, raw edges. Wool trousers.
Photographer: Christian Friis, Model: Maja Krag

:: Sculptural
dress in jersey
coated neoprene.
*Photographer:
Christian Friis, Model:
Maja Krag*

:: Sheer silk blouse.
Skirt in jersey
coated neoprene.
*Photographer:
Christian Friis, Model:
Maja Krag*

:: Sculptural wool
coat. *Photographer:
Christian Friis, Model:
Maja Krag*

:: Top in heavy
wool. Trousers in thin
wool. *Photographer:
Christian Friis, Model:
Maja Krag*

MAGNUS LÖPPE

**Fashion Design BA
TEKO**
Home town/Country:
Hiiumaa, Estonia

Inspiration:
001 – The Deforming
Project is inspired by
French-Hungarian
photographer Lucien
Hervé's work, and is
about reinterpreting
traditional menswear,
playing with quilting,
layers, clean lines,
uncommon silhouettes,
and forms.
Further concept
description at www.
magnusloppe.com

Graduation/Awards:
Designers' Nest Award
winner, Copenhagen
Fashion Week,
February 2010

Advised by:
Ike Rust,
    Senior Tutor at Royal
    College of Art,
    London;
Jens Laugesen,
    Designer

Garment – Three armhole jacket. *Images by Michael Hansen,
www.michaelhansenwork.dk, model, Benyamin A*

:: Garment – Three armhole jacket. *Images by Michael Hansen, www. michaelhansenwork. dk, model, Benyamin A*

:: Garment – Three armhole heavy coat. *Images by Michael Hansen, www. michaelhansenwork. dk, model, Benyamin A*

:: Garment – The cocoon jacket. *Images by Michael Hansen, www. michaelhansenwork. dk, model, Benyamin A*

:: Garment – One button continuing shirt. *Images by Michael Hansen, www. michaelhansenwork. dk, model, Benyamin A*

TANNE VINTER

Design Business, VIA University College TEKO

Home town/Country: Aarhus, Denmark

Design Fashion

Inspiration:
An interpretation and fusion between art and the essential elements of our existence.
Christo's fascinating packaging techniques used in his contemporary art installations, revealing wrapped unpredictable silhouettes.
Richard Serra's minimalistic, abstract, and process-based sculptures. Hard yet soft, rigorous yet organic.
The body, the heat, the vitality, the movement, the impulses, the intense development of life.
Compacted body postures from a vulnerable untouched organism–a fragile foetus.
A clean, minimalist manifestation, where complex simplicity arises.

Graduation/Awards:
Finalist, "Designers Nest"—Copenhagen Fashion Week 2011
Talent scholarship from TEKO

Advised by:
Birgitta Johanson, Designer, TEKO-VIA.
Jens Laugesen, Designer

Gauze wool/silk dress. Photographer: Mumilab / Peter Ravnsborg, Model: 2pm/Pernille Møller, Stylist: Divamodels / Marianne Lind

146

:: Heavy wool coat.
*Photographer:
Mumilab / Peter
Ravnsborg, Model:
2pm/Pernille Møller,
Stylist: Divamodels /
Marianne Lind*

:: Loosely woven
silk-cotton mix blouse.
*Photographer:
Mumilab / Peter
Ravnsborg, Model:
2pm/Pernille Møller,
Stylist: Divamodels /
Marianne Lind*

:: Lamb leather
jacket. Cotton
organza trousers.
*Photographer:
Mumilab / Peter
Ravnsborg, Model:
2pm/Pernille Møller,
Stylist: Divamodels /
Marianne Lind*

:: Silk dress.
*Photographer:
Mumilab / Peter
Ravnsborg, Model:
2pm/Pernille Møller,
Stylist: Divamodels /
Marianne Lind*

LYNSEY CAMPBELL

**BA Performance
Sportswear Design
University College
Falmouth**
Home town/Country:
Leigh, England

Graduation/Awards:
PSD award for
excellence presented
by Finisterre

Advised by:
Mr. John Boddy;
Mrs. Jane Gotellier;
Mr. Tom Podkilinski

Printed jacket with taped seams and glow in the dark
properties (fabric Energlo) with printed mesh shorts. Tape
seamed, mesh panel 3/4 leggings and glow in the dark,
printed tabard. Design by Lynsey Campbell.
Photo by William Rouse

148

:::: Printed tabard
(fabric energlo) with
mesh panelled ¾
leggings with flat
glued seams. Design
by Lynsey Campbell.
Photo by
William Rouse

:::: Sophie Anderton
in mesh printed white
leotard with hidden
bust support. Design
by Lynsey Campbell.
Photo by
William Rouse

JACK GULLACHSEN

**Fashion Design
BA (Honors)
University
College Falmouth**
Home town/Country:
Warwickshire, United
Kingdom

Menswear

Inspiration:
Inspired by my own lost
family heritage for Norway,
being lost both literally
and metaphorically,
and my great, great
Grandfather's bespoke
furniture label. Also
applying the silhouette
of soft tailoring and
aesthetical theory of
Wabi Sabi.

Graduation/Awards:
First Class BA HONS
Winner of live design
    and construction
    project with Luella
    Bartley and Tanya
    Sarne

Photography: Lorentz Gullachsen, Model: Tuner Moyse

:: *Photography:*
Lorentz Gullachsen,
Model: Tuner Moyse

:: *Photography:*
Lorentz Gullachsen,
Model: Tuner Moyse

:: *Photography:*
Lorentz Gullachsen,
Model: Tuner Moyse

:: *Photography:*
Lorentz Gullachsen,
Model: Tuner Moyse

SOPHIE HAWKINS

**BA Hons
Fashion Design
University College
Falmouth**
Home town/Country:
Somerset, UK

**Ethical and
Functional Menswear**

Inspiration:
Sophie Hawkins has a unique eco-innovative approach to menswear design. Encapsulating her love for the outdoors, sports and exploring other cultures, her menswear collections demonstrate ethical, ergonomic clothing with energetic style. Her collection for her own "Shiny Jacket Company" demonstrates builder's functional clothing, alternatively using only re-claimed fabrics in bold, naturally dyed colours.

Graduation/Awards:
Winner of the Cooperative Bank's Ethical Award for most ethical collection.

Advised by:
Bridget Woods Kramer

Orange outfit: Workman's parka: made of wool, naturally dyed with madder. With fish skin panels on the shoulders and back. Trousers: made from reclaimed rip-stop nylon parachute, ultra sewn with heat weld seams. *Illustration by Sophie Hawkins: www.23withamoneytree.tumblr.com*

:: Orange outfit: Workman's parka: made of wool, naturally dyed with madder. With fish skin panels on the shoulders and back. Trousers: made from reclaimed rip-stop nylon parachute, ultra sewn with heat weld seams. *Photography by Sophie Turner: www.boxhand.co.uk*

:: Blue outfit: waterproof parka made in: blue re-claimed nylon parachute , screen printed with wide stripes, fish skin storm flap and re-used reflective strip seams. Hi-vis jeans made of: re-cycled garments, died with natural indigo with use of re-claimed reflective strips. *Illustration by Sophie Hawkins: www.23withamoneytree.tumblr.com*

.:: Waterproof parka made in: blue re-claimed nylon parachute , screen printed, fish skin storm flap and re-used reflective strip seams. Hi-vis jeans made of: re-cycled garments, died with natural indigo with use of re-claimed reflective strips. *Photography by Sophie Turner: www.boxhand.co.uk*

ANNALEIGH HOCKADAY

BA (Hons)
Performance
Sportswear Design
University College
Falmouth
Home town/Country:
Devon, United Kingdom

Inspiration:
Mantol, meaning "balance" in the Cornish language, is an organic and fair trade collection derived from the love of the Devon and Cornish coastline whilst studying traditional trades and crafts that have developed in these ruggedly, beautiful places. The aim was to balance the masculine and feminine and develop technical performance with timeless style.

Graduation/Awards:
Runner up for the David Nieper Award 2011.
Winner of the Sorrell Award 2001 for dedication to studies and outstanding academic achievement.

Advised by:
Jane Gottelier, Course Leader;
Thomas Podkolinski, Tutor

CHLOE REYNOLDS

**Fashion Design
(BA Hons)
University
College Falmouth**
Home town/Country:
Sussex, England

**Experimental
Pattern Cutting**

Inspiration:
This futuristic and apocalypse-inspired collection is based on survival and protection, focusing on animal armor such as armadillo shells and fish scales. It is constructed from entirely black fabrics, and incorporates intricate laser cut and anodized metal embellishments.

Graduation/Awards:
Sri Lanka Design Festival award in the Swimwear category (May 2010)

Advised by:
Jane Gottelier

Wool jumpsuit with structured back panels, magnet fastenings, and fixed rubber belt.
Photography by Charlotte Aikon

:: Lamb nappa leather armadillo jacket with sheepskin-lined hood, and viscose lycra and rubber panelled skirt. *Photography by Charlotte Aiken*

:: Silk chiffon and leather panelled dress, lycra twisted leg jumpsuit, and shoes from recycled record shards. *Photography by Charlotte Aiken*

:: High waisted cotton trousers hand embellished with laser cut anodized aluminium sequins. *Photography by Charlotte Aiken*

:: Indian ink hand illustration of graduate collection.

JOSS BURNELL

**MDes Fashion with
Business Studies
University of Brighton**
Home town/Country:
Wimbledon, UK

Inspiration:
This autumn/winter
menswear collection
explores the realities
of modern day
British suburbia,
drawing inspiration
from photographic
documentation and
personal reflections. A
preoccupation with the
mundane revealed itself
as a prevailing theme,
and from this an overriding
mood and atmosphere
becomes the driving
force behind my work.
Oversized silhouettes and
exaggerated proportions,
contributing to a sense of
awkwardness, mirror the
captivating peculiarity
I experienced from
suburban living.

Graduation/Awards:
Santander Award
    for Excellence and
    Achievement in Arts
    and Design
Nagoya University Prize
    in recognition of
    outstanding artistic
    achievement

Advised by:
Malcolm McInnes:
    Course Leader;
Jane Shepherd:
    Course Tutor

Cotton satin oversized coat with handcrafted giant metal
hood and eye fastening. *Photo by Joe Williams,
Model: John Holt*

:: Brick knit oversized square jumper with cotton voile granddad shirt and jersey rib long johns. *Photo by Joe Williams, model John Holt*

:: Nappa leather yoke wool shirt jacket with mustard rib jumper and pebble dash wool wide leg trousers. *Photo by Joe Williams, model John Holt*

:: Extra long ribbed jersey top with high waisted exaggerated wide leg wool trouser with handmade leather belt. *Photo by Joe Williams, model John Holt*

:: Distressed felt woven wrap with mustard knit and jersey long johns. *Photo by Joe Williams, model John Holt*

GRANT DURRELL

**MDes Fashion Design
with Business Studies
University of Brighton**
Home town/Country:
London, England

Pattern cutting

Inspiration:
Medical photography
and the works of Andreas
Vesalius. Manipulating
the female form through
innovative pattern
cutting to give the
wearer a new clothing
experience.

Advised by:
Malcolm McInness
and Gael Mailhol

*Silk zibeline jacket and silk jersey tube skirt. Hood and jacket
all one piece. Photography by fashionshowimages.com*

:: Leather and silk cotton top and silk zibeline humped skirt. One sleeve eliminated on top. Hump in skirt created by melting and shaping wadding. *Photography by fashionshowimages. com*

:: Short mohair bodice with goat hair sleeves. *Photography by fashionshowimages. com*

:: Leather and goat hair jackel and silk jersey skirt– both sleeves eliminated. *Photography by fashionshowimages. com*

:: Goat hair jacket and silk jersey skirt. Humped shoulder created by melting and shaping wadding. *Photography by fashionshowimages. com*

LAURA WALDEN

MDes Fashion with Business Studies University of Brighton
Home town/Country: Sherston, Wiltshire

Inspiration:
Inspired by the industrial documentary photographic works of Bern & Hilla Becher, this womenswear collection is motivated by function, construction, and understated yet assured design. Ultimately, the collection is shaped by the paradoxical complexity and simplicity of the garments, defined by humble processes that creatively enquire into intellectual cutting and construction.

Advised by:
Malcolm McInnes: Principal Fashion Lecturer, University of Brighton

Nylon shirt over cotton jersey dress. *Photography by Bob Seager – The University of Brighton*

:: Striped cotton shirt over wool/cashmere trousers. *Photography by Bob Seager – The University of Brighton*

:: Waxed cotton coat over cotton jersey dress.

:: Cotton sateen shirt over wool/cashmere trousers.

:: Linen coat over striped cotton shirt dress.

KATY MCGUIRK

Fashion Design with Textiles BA (Hons) University of Huddersfield
Home town/Country: Ormskirk, UK

Fashion Design with Textiles

Graduation/Awards:
First prize in the Worldskills Made to Measure UK Finals Design Competition 2008

Reconstructed Jacket with external lining, paired with fine linen knit midi length dress with acid underlayer.
Final Collection - Spring Summer 2012

Mixed media, hand drawn with pencil, pencil crayon, and Photoshop.

Fine jersey knit polo shirt with side collar feature and draped sleeves, paired with silk midi skirt with curved gathered waist band

Moulded oversized tunic in floral printed satin. Paired with gathered pale grey powernet skirt.

:: Mixed media, hand drawn with pencil, pencil crayon, and Photoshop

:: Mixed media, hand drawn with pencil, pencil crayon, and Photoshop

.:: Hand drawn and Photoshop print

KATY MCGUIRK

BECKY MILNE

Fashion Design with Textiles BA (Hons) University of Huddersfield

Home town/Country: Newry, CO.DOWN

Fashion Design with Textiles

Inspiration:

The idea behind the collection was taken from sandstorms; the strength and unforgiving nature seen in their appearance and overpowering force, yet they resemble and leave behind a blurred softness. The muted black figures found in images of the dustbowls are key to this semi-transparent, predominantly black collection. Pleated layers with hidden embroidered beading add depth and a sense of wonder, as seen in dust clouds, a kind of lucrative secret to what is hidden underneath.

Torn Visibility.
a.w 12

'Zip my head in' dress & 'Leave my head out of it' jacket

Mixed media, Photoshop, pencil, water color.

Torn Visibility.
a.w 12

'Trailing behind me' shirt & 'Chain reaction' pant

Torn Visibility.
a.w 12

'Heads up' jacket and 'Sling your hook' dress

:: Mixed media,
Photoshop, pencil,
water color.

:: Mixed media,
Photoshop, pencil,
water color.

:: Illustrator

:: Illustrator

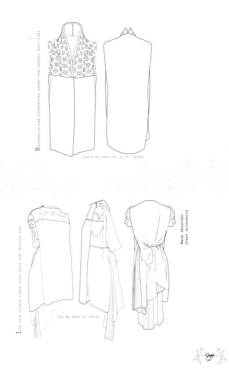

NICOLA BREAM

BA Hons
Fashion & Design
University of Salford
Home town/Country:
Conwy, Wales, UK

Inspiration:
I decided to base my collection on the Constructivist movement of the early twentieth century. I was inspired by futurism, geometric structures, unique shapes, and abstract art. Artists such as Tatin, Rodchenko, Stepanovand, Sonia Delauney, and Rodolf Paglialunga also influenced my ideas.

OLIVIA GRACE DEENEY

University of Salford
Home town/Country:
Manchester, England

Fashion Design:
Womenswear

Inspiration:
Inspired by the human act of hoarding. Objects are emotion holders; they mean little when we return to dust. She is the Angel of History, walking backwards into the future, surveying hoarded possessions behind her. There is an overall essence of aging and distress to represent the transience of time. As it sweeps and curves, taking over the wearer's body and mind, slowly engulfing them. It represents "the obsession." Made from hand dyed goose feathers and tulle with hook and eye back fasteners. *Photography by Layla Sailor Photography*

As it sweeps and curves, taking over the wearer's body and mind, slowly engulfing them. It represents "the obsession." Made from hand dyed goose feathers and tulle with hook and eye back fasteners.
Photography by Layla Sailor Photography

:: The delicate chiffon collects objects that feed her fixation. Her body exudes the overwhelming power of the obsession, and it seeps down the dress displaying sick, yet beautiful ornate embellishment. Made from French silk chiffon with the top half dipped in liquid latex. The under slip is printed silk replica of the tapestry. And the embellishment is metal chain, chandelier beads, and magpie wings. *Photography by Layla Sailor Photography*

:: Made from power net and furnishing beads attached using jewelry techniques with a hook and eye back fastening. *Photography by Layla Sailor Photography*

:: The tapestry reminded her of her grandmother's old worn reading chair. The musky smell she would inhale as a child. Instantly there was a connection, and she had to have it. *Photography by Layla Sailor Photography*

:: Dress made by furnishing leather and delicate French lace with heavy satchel fastening buckles at back. Jacket made from French silk chiffon fully dipped in liquid latex with velvet bound edges. Headdress made from same leather as dress with velvet bound edges and chandelier embellishments. *Photography by Layla Sailor Photography*

GEORGIA RHIANE THORNE

BA (Hons)
Fashion Design
University
of Salford
Home town/Country:
Manchester, England

Fashion Design

Inspiration:
Inspired by the street artist, Richard Hambleton, and his *Shadowman* collection. I have looked into shadows, the shapes, feelings, and mood surrounding. Leading me to create a luxurious, black and white collection of pieces portraying the light with the shadow, which follows.

Graduation/Awards:
BA Honors First Class Degree in Fashion Design.

Photography by Simon Armstrong

:: *Photography by
Simon Armstrong*

:: *Photography by
Simon Armstrong*

:: *Illustration by
Georgia Thorne*

:: *Illustration by
Georgia Thorne*

CHARLOTTE WATERS

**Fashion Design
BA (Hons)
University
of Salford**
Home town/Country:
Bradford, England

**Womenswear,
knitwear**

Inspiration:
I was inspired by today's technology and how it has evolved since I was a child. I wanted to take old, unwanted, obsolete, technology of the past and make it desirable once more in an elegant and innovative way.

Graduation/Awards:
Nominated for Stuart Peters Visionary Knitwear award.
Finalist in UK hand knitting and textile award.
Harvey Nichols Award for best womenswear collection 2011.

Advised by:
Bashur Aswat,
Head of Fashion and Design and Course Leader at the University of Salford.

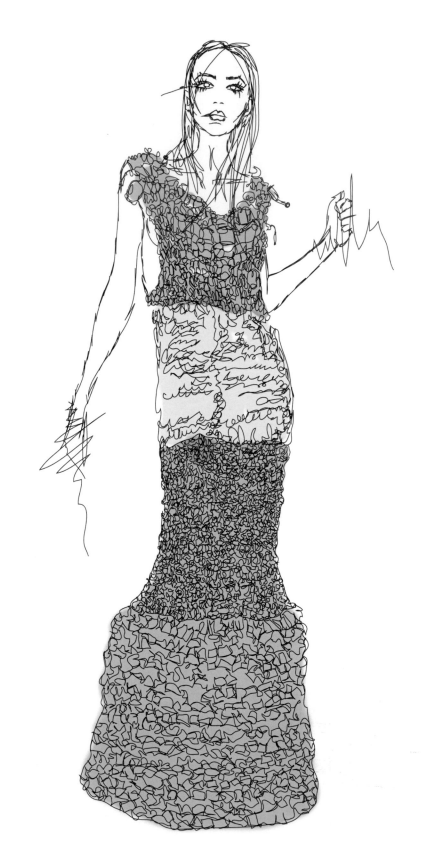

Free hand illustration. *Illustration by Charlotte Waters*

:: Free hand illustration. *Illustration by Charlotte Waters*

:: Free hand illustration. *Illustration by Charlotte Waters*

:: Hand knitted show piece made from old wires, adapters, video tape and vinyl fused felt. *Photography by Simon Armstrong*

:: Hand knitted jacket made from video tape and Merino wool yarn with a metal silk dress. *Photography by Simon Armstrong*

JAYNE BRISTOW

BDes (Hons)
Textiles and Fashion
University of Ulster
Home town/Country:
Northern Ireland

Fashion and Knit

Inspiration:
The collection *Ndebele* is inspired by the colorful mix of South African culture, patterns and textures. The vibrant use of jewel colors and the development of digital prints, embroideries and knitwear reflect the wonderful textiles used and reused in that region.

Advised by:
Mrs Alison Gault:
  Course Director;
Ms Janet Coulter:
  Senior Lecturer

Felted dress with hand embroidered beads, double-bed coat knitted in Jacquard and tuck stitched in merino wool.
Photography by University of Ulster

:: Felt coat and velvet dress with beaded neck detail. *Photography by University of Ulster*

:: Felt coat and velvet dress with beaded neck detail. *Photography by University of Ulster*

:: Felt coat with embroidery detail in front panel. *Photography by University of Ulster*

ASHLEE COBURN

**BDes (Hons)
Textiles and Fashion
University of Ulster**
Home town/Country:
Northern Ireland

Fashion and Knit

Inspiration:
Henna tattoos and
the inspiration of the
East, filigree windows
with peacock feathers
and gilt stone buildings,
saris lightly covering
the female form were
developed into prints,
embroideries, and
knitwear.

Advised by:
Mrs Alison Gault:
   Course Director;
Ms Janet Coulter:
   Senior Lecturer

Embroidered, cutwork fabric with light beading.
Photography by University of Ulster

:: Digital print and leather short sleeve jacket. *Photography by University of Ulster*

:: Embroidered, cutwork fabric with light beading, silk scarf. *Photography by University of Ulster*

:: Knitted jacket with lace, Fair Isle, digital print scarf, silk embroidered top, silk and wool trousers. *Photography by University of Ulster*

:: Knitted jacket with lace, Fair Isle, digital print scarf, silk embroidered top, silk and wool trousers. *Photography by University of Ulster*

RACHEL SHAW

BDes (Hons)
Textiles and Fashion
University of Ulster
Home town/Country:
Northern Ireland

Fashion and Knit

Inspiration:
Inspiration was based on the Barbary pirates, shipwrecks, beach combing, and coastal cavernous caves. Washed out, distressed, and dip dying created fabrics reflecting the theme. Knitwear created with space dyed chunky yarns, the mainly grey hues were lifted with flashes of magenta, lime, and chalky whites.

Graduation/Awards:
House of Fraser
Project Protégé

Advised by:
Mrs Alison Gault:
    Course Director;
Ms Janet Coulter:
    Senior Lecturer

Suede hooded loose fitting shirt with knitted gilet with hand inlay mohair. *Photography by University of Ulster*

:: Faux fur jacket, jersey leggings, and hand dyed jersey top. *Photography by University of Ulster*

:: Leather hotpants with hand dyed top and microfiber cardigan. *Photography by University of Ulster*

:: Italian microfiber cardigan with flashes of magenta, sulphur, and chalky greys. *Photography by University of Ulster*

:: Faux fur jacket, jersey leggings, and hand dyed jersey top. *Photography by University of Ulster*

PARSHA GERAYESH

**BA (Hons)
Fashion Design
University of
Westminster**
Home town/Country:
UK

Womenswear

Inspiration:
Entitled 455,638,
the collection is an
exploration into new forms
of garment construction.
The title is a six-figure grid
reference for my house
where the concept was
conceived.
Visualized sound patterns
based on cymatic
interpretations of the
title are projected on to
the body consequently
directing the silhouette
and design of each
garment.

Graduation/Awards:
Hammerson Innovation
    Award – Graduate
    Fashion Week 2011
Chosen For Vauxhall
    Fashion Scout
    Ba Showcase
    September 2011

Advised by:
Andrew Groves:
Course Director.

Steam bent beech frame with elastic weave
Hand carved laminated wool felt skirt.
Photography by Chris Moore, Catwalking

:: Faux fur jacket, jersey leggings, and hand dyed jersey top. *Photography by University of Ulster*

:: Leather hotpants with hand dyed top and microfiber cardigan. *Photography by University of Ulster*

:: Italian microfiber cardigan with flashes of magenta, sulphur, and chalky greys. *Photography by University of Ulster*

:: Faux fur jacket, jersey leggings, and hand dyed jersey top. *Photography by University of Ulster*

KRYSTYNA SCULLION

BDes (Hons)
Textiles and Fashion
University of Ulster
Home town/Country:
Northern Ireland

Fashion and Knit

Inspiration:
The design inspiration stems from childhood memories after a visit to the V & A Museum. Krystyna looked retrospectively at the clothes, toys, and all the memorabilia in the '80s and brought a new fun to her fashion designs with an eclectic mix of images, materials, and shapes.

Advised by:
Mrs Alison Gault:
    Course Director;
Ms Janet Coulter:
    Senior Lecturer

Coated linen A line dress, PVC collar, felted knitwear also incorporates intarsia and appliqué.
Photography by University of Ulster

:: Evolon pinafore, multicolored Fair Isles knitwear and cotton shirt with ribbon. *Photography by University of Ulster*

:: *Photography by University of Ulster*

:: PVC raincoat, with digital print design on knitted Jersey Jump suit. *Photography by University of Ulster*

:: PVC raincoat, with digital print design on knitted Jersey Jump suit. *Photography by University of Ulster*

PARSHA GERAYESH

**BA (Hons)
Fashion Design
University of
Westminster**
Home town/Country:
UK

Womenswear

Inspiration:
Entitled 455,638,
the collection is an
exploration into new forms
of garment construction.
The title is a six-figure grid
reference for my house
where the concept was
conceived.
Visualized sound patterns
based on cymatic
interpretations of the
title are projected on to
the body consequently
directing the silhouette
and design of each
garment.

Graduation/Awards:
Hammerson Innovation
Award – Graduate
Fashion Week 2011
Chosen For Vauxhall
Fashion Scout
Ba Showcase
September 2011

Advised by:
Andrew Groves:
Course Director.

Steam bent beech frame with elastic weave.
Hand carved laminated wool felt skirt.
Photography by Chris Moore, Catwalking

190

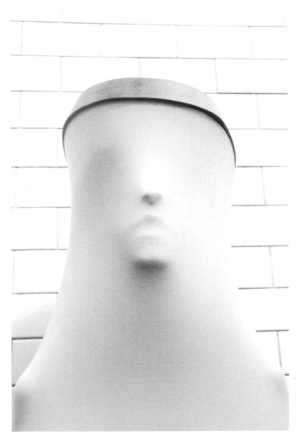

:: Navy Silk contour projection pattern dress. Steam bent beech frame with cream stretched silk jersey. *Photography by Chris Moore, Catwalking*

:: Steam bent beech frame with grey stretched/draped wool. *Photography by Chris Moore, Catwalking*

:: Steam bent beech frame with white stretched silk jersey. *Photography by Alis Pelleschi*

:: Steam bent beech frame with grey stretched cashmere wool. *Photography by Alis Pelleschi*

OLIVIA HANSON

**BA (Hons)
Fashion Design
University of
Westminster**
Home town/Country:
London, UK

Womenswear

Inspiration:
The study of air and
the absence of air in
inflatables.

Graduation/Awards:
Shortlisted for
Graduate Fashion
Week's Accessories
Award by Mulberry

Advised by:
Andrew Groves:
Course Director.

Giraffe jacket is made from a silk screen
printed satin and put with screen printed jersey
leggings and has been stuffed to create fullness.
The shoes are covered with a recycled inflatable octopus.
Photography by Christopher Moore, catwalking.com

:: The front view of the inflatable crocodile. The lining garment is made from a silk screen printed satin and the inflated outer is made from an ultrasonically welded PVC, which has been hand colored with a black marker pen and has been inflated by a battery powered fan that continuously pumps air through the garment, allowing it to inflate. The shoes are covered with a recycled inflatable crocodile. *Photography by Christopher Moore, catwalking.com*

:: The back view of the inflatable crocodile. *Photography by Christopher Moore, catwalking.com*

:: The lining garment is made from a silk screen printed organza and the inflated outer is made from an ultrasonically welded PVC which has been hand colored with a black marker pen and has been inflated by a battery powered fan that continuously pumps air through the garment allowing it to inflate. *Photography by Christopher Moore, catwalking.com*

:: The lining garment is made from a silk screen printed satin and the inflated outer is made from an ultrasonically welded PVC which has been hand colored with a black marker pen and has been inflated by a battery powered fan that continuously pumps air through the garment allowing it to inflate. *Photography by Christopher Moore, catwalking.com*

LAURA JOYNER

**BA (Hons)
Fashion Design
University of
Westminster**
Home town/Country:
London, UK

Womenswear

Inspiration:
My research started
with Oscar Marzaroli's
book *Shades of Grey*.
His photographs of
the Gorbals in 1970s
Glasgow were of
real people—from
children playing to
washerwomen working
in the steamies. I
developed textiles that
played on tradition and
would make people
question how they were
made. I applied these in
wearable garments for
a modern woman.

Graduation/Awards:
Shortlisted—David
  Band Textile Award
  GFW 2011
Attending CSM for
  Womenswear MA in
  the Autumn
Chosen for MaxMara's
  Young Designer's
  showroom in July

Advised by:
Andrew Groves:
Course Director.

Needle punched wool and latex jacket with
sequin facing. Screen printed kilt. Sequinned top.
Photography by Chris Moore, catwalking.com

:: Needle punched wool and latex jacket with Merino hand knit rib. Color changing foiled latex crop top. Screen printed sequin and leather skirt. *Photography by Chris Moore, catwalking.com*

:: Color changing foiled Merino bobble jumper. Hand cut lace edge and screen printed latex skirt. *Photography by Chris Moore, catwalking.com*

:: Needle punched wool and latex coat with sequin collar. Color changing foiled Merino cable knit. Screen printed pleated skirt. *Photography by Chris Moore, catwalking.com*

:: Hand cut lace edge and screen printed latex dress. Sequin and leather skirt. *Photography by Chris Moore, catwalking.com*

MOLLY MCCUTCHEON

BA (Hons)
Fashion Design
University of
Westminster
Home town/Country:
UK

Menswear

Inspiration:
My collection is about capturing all the spirit of a fantastic Riviera holiday in the 1930s, but with the striking '30s menswear silhouettes given ultra modern details, finishes, and vivid hand-dye techniques. I kept all garments white to echo the loose white linen attire often sported by the stylish '30s holidaymakers, but also to act as a blank canvas to my hand-sprayed artist-inspired dye work.

Advised by:
Andrew Groves:
Course Director.

Lightweight cotton blend drape-pocket jacket. Cotton blend box pleat front trousers with hand-dyed lower half. Collarless cotton shirt with hidden-button placket. Knotted cord belt with white leather detailing. Reverse dye bag with white polyester mesh layer, canvas panelling, leather detailing, and cord/leather accessory. *Photography by Chris Moore*

:: Sweatshirt jersey top with hand-dyed section and cotton drill panel at bottom. Sheer cotton organza box pleat shorts. Silk jersey t-shirt (underneath). *Photography by Chris Moore*

:: Cotton drill jacket with hand-dyed top half. Airtex lining. Half coarse linen half polyester box pleat trousers with raw-edge detail at knee. Cotton shirt with hidden-button placket. Knotted cord belt with white leather detailing. *Photography by Chris Moore*

:: Sweatshirt jersey top with wool felt panel and side pocket detail. Cotton drill trousers with all-over hand-dye on reverse side (for subtle effect). Knotted cord belt with white leather detailing. Cotton shirt with hidden-button placket. *Photography by Chris Moore*

:: Sweatshirt jersey tight t-shirt with hand-dye section. Half Irish linen half hand-crinkled cotton blend trousers. Cotton shirt with hidden-button placket. Knotted cord belt with white leather detailing. *Photography by Chris Moore*

KATE WALLIS

**BA (Hons)
Fashion Design
University of
Westminster**
Home town/Country:
London, UK

Womenswear

Inspiration:
The origins of my research for my final collection lie in the attitude of the woman I was designing for; confident, sexy and with a slight edge. I selected luxury fabrics including Origin Assured fox fur, 24 carat gold-plated metal pieces and couture fabrics from Switzerland. Using the hard metals with the fur creates a new aesthetic for a material currently enjoying a modern revival. The tailored silhouette with beautiful fabrications of sequins against the exaggerated extravagance of the fur jackets creates an aesthetic that means the Kate Wallis woman will never go unnoticed.

Graduation/Awards:
University of
Westminster
Silver Scholarship

Advised by:
Andrew Groves:
Course Director.

Fox and rabbit fur jacket with 24ct gold metal pieces.
Multi-color hand-sequinned bandeau dress.
copyright © 2010 Christopher Moore Limited

:: Toscana wool, feather, and chiffon skirt dress with 24ct gold neck plate. *copyright © 2010 Christopher Moore Limited*

:: Blue ostrich feather and gunmetal leather dress. *copyright © 2010 Christopher Moore Limited*

:: Fox and rabbit fur jumper with 24ct gold cuffs and sequinned hotpants. *copyright © 2010 Christopher Moore Limited*

:: Gold hand-sequinned, ostrich and pheasant feather dress with 24ct gold metal shoulder pieces. *copyright © 2010 Christopher Moore Limited*